For Parents: Introduction

Why this Workbook?

We believe kids get better at math with practice, resulting in confidence and positive attitude towards math that is required to excel in school.

This workbook provides kids with additional math practice that reinforces and complements what is taught at school. There are no pictures or word problems, and focus on mastery of basic addition and subtraction.

This workbook combines traditional addition and subtraction math problems, with number bond problems. Many elementary schools teach math using Number Bonds, and we want kids to have practice on both traditional math questions and number bonds to build fluency and speed in basic arithmetic.

What is a Number Bond?

A Number Bond is a visual representation of the relationship between addition and subtraction, showing the biggest number (the "whole") is made up of 2 smaller numbers (the "parts").

Why Number Bond?

Number bond is a great way for kids to practice addition and subtraction concepts. It helps kids break down math problems into smaller pieces and see the relationship between numbers. It also allows kids to see the inverse relationship between addition and subtraction. Subtraction also becomes easier after number bond practice.

Addition / Subtraction

Additional Benefits to Number Bonds -- Algebraic Thinking

Practicing with number bonds help kids get ready for algebra later on. When they look at a basic equation, they can recognize which of the numbers is the "whole" — the number at the top of the number bond — based on its position in the equation.

Example: x + 1 = 3

Kids who are used to number bonds can visualize a number bond with the "3" on top and "1" in one of the circles at the bottom, and algebra will be easier when they get to it a few years later.

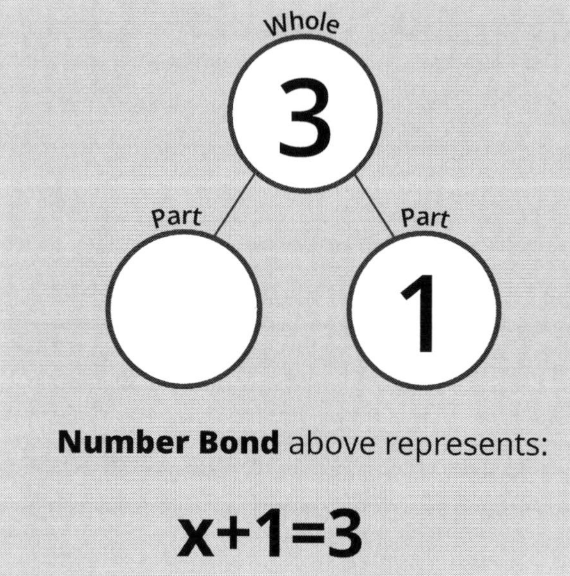

How to Get Your Kid to Practice Math
More math practice will increase math fluency and speed, resulting in math confidence. But how do we get our kids to sit down and do math worksheets?

Create a Habit of Math Practice
All habits can be broken down into: 1) Cue or Trigger, 2) Routine, 3) Reward.

Turning math practice into a habit is figuring out what kind of cue/reward you would like to create for your child, and works for you and your family.

Examples:
- Kid comes home (cue), math practice (routine), get a snack (reward)
- Kid finishes snack (cue), does 3 pages (routine), gets 3 stickers (reward)
- Kid finishes dinner (cue), math practice (routine), dessert (reward)
- Kid finishes snack after school (cue), math practice - 5 pages (routine), screen time for 10 minutes (reward)

Progress Chart

When a page is completed, add a sticker or smiley face to a square below. When the whole chart is completed, you would have completed 100 pages!

If you have feedback, questions, or would like a printable pdf of pages you like in the book, email us at mathbook1@numberbondgames.com

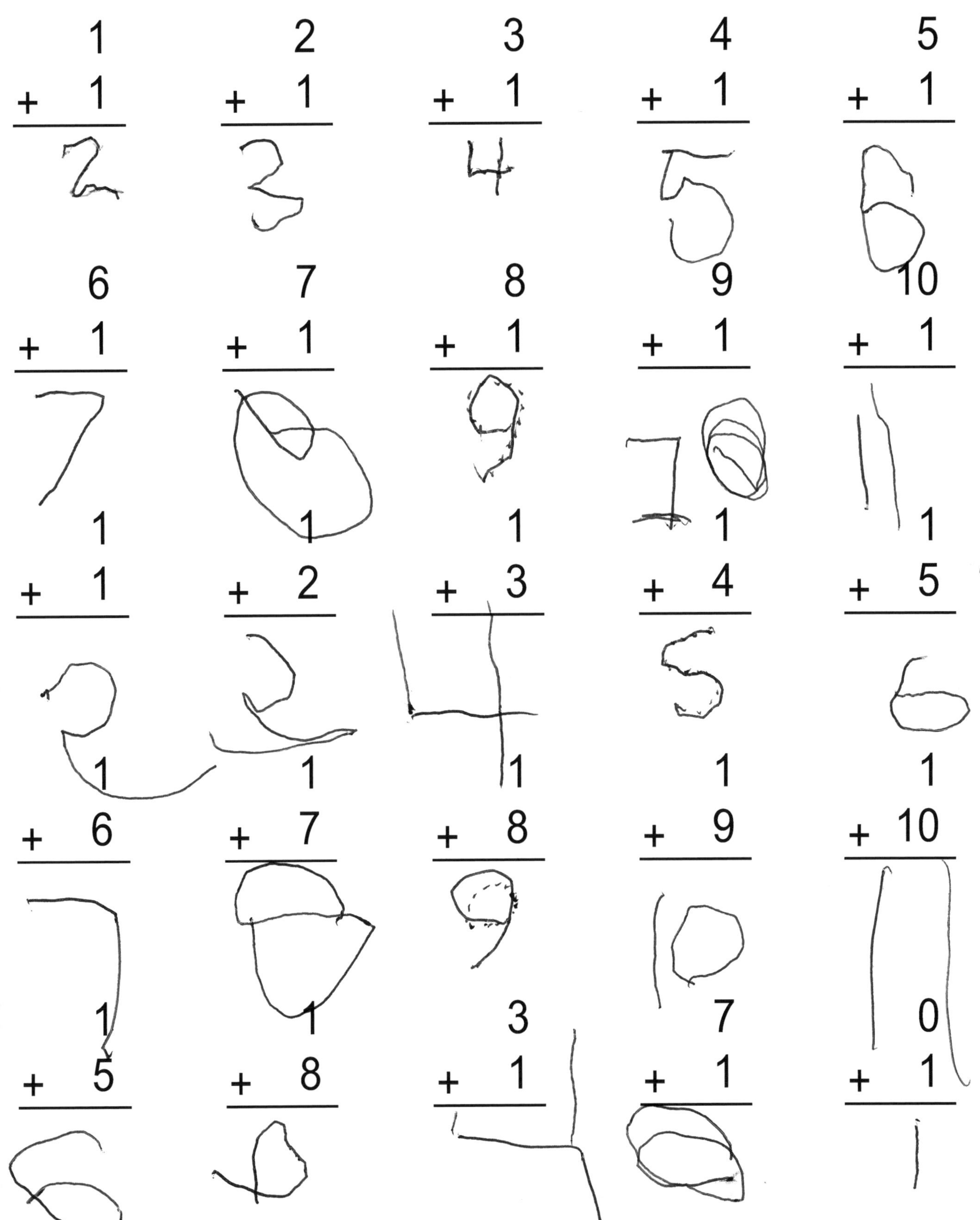
1 + 1
2 + 1
3 + 1
4 + 1
5 + 1
6 + 1
7 + 1
8 + 1
9 + 1
10 + 1
1 + 1
1 + 2
1 + 3
1 + 4
1 + 5
1 + 6
1 + 7
1 + 8
1 + 9
1 + 10
1 + 5
1 + 8
3 + 1
7 + 1
0 + 1

2
1
1
2
1
1
3
1
2
4
1
3
8
1
7
1
1
0
5
1
4
6
5
1
1
100
99
1
1000
999
1
2000
1,999
1

$1 + \boxed{2}$ → 1 + 1 = [2]

1 + [1] = 2

[2] + 1 = 3

2 + 1 = [3]

1 + [3] = 4

[2] + 1 = 3

3 + 1 = [4]

1 + [4] = 5

[4] + 1 = 5

1 + 4 = [5]

6 + [1] = 7

[1] + 5 = 6

8 + 1 = [9]

1 + 9 = [10]

1 + 2	2 + 2	3 + 2	4 + 2	5 + 2
Answer: 3	Answer: 4	Answer: 5	Answer: 6	Answer: 7
6 + 2	7 + 2	8 + 2	9 + 2	10 + 2
Answer: 8	Answer: 9	Answer: 10	Answer: 11	Answer: 12
2 + 1	2 + 2	2 + 3	2 + 4	2 + 5
Answer: 3	Answer: 4	Answer: 5	Answer: 6	Answer: 7
2 + 6	2 + 7	2 + 8	2 + 9	2 + 10
Answer: 8	Answer: 9	Answer: 10	Answer: 11	Answer: 12
2 + 5	2 + 8	3 + 2	7 + 2	9 + 2
Answer: 7	Answer: 10	Answer: 5	Answer: 9	Answer: 11

3
1
2
3
1
2
4
2
2
5
2
3
8
2
6
6
2
4
7
2
5
8
6
2
10
2
8
1,002
1000
2
3
1
2
2002
2000
2

$2 + 1 = \boxed{3}$

$2 + \boxed{1} = 3$

$\boxed{2} + 2 = 4$

$2 + 2 = \boxed{4}$

$2 + \boxed{3} = 5$

$\boxed{1} + 2 = 3$

$3 + 2 = \boxed{5}$

$2 + \boxed{4} = 6$

$\boxed{5} + 2 = 7$

$2 + 4 = \boxed{6}$

$6 + \boxed{2} = 8$

$\boxed{2} + 5 = 7$

$8 + 2 = \boxed{10}$

$2 + 9 = \boxed{11}$

Adding 3

1 + 3 = 4	3 + 2 = 5	3 + 3 = 6	4 + 3 = 7	5 + 3 = 8
6 + 3 = 9	7 + 3 = 10	8 + 3 = 11	9 + 3 = 12	10 + 3 = 13
3 + 1 = 4	3 + 2 = 5	3 + 3 = 6	3 + 4 = 7	3 + 5 = 8
3 + 6 = 9	3 + 7 = 10	3 + 8 = 11	3 + 9 = 12	3 + 10 = 13
3 + 5 = 8	3 + 8 = 11	3 + 3 = 6	7 + 3 = 10	9 + 3 = 12

Number Bonds: 3

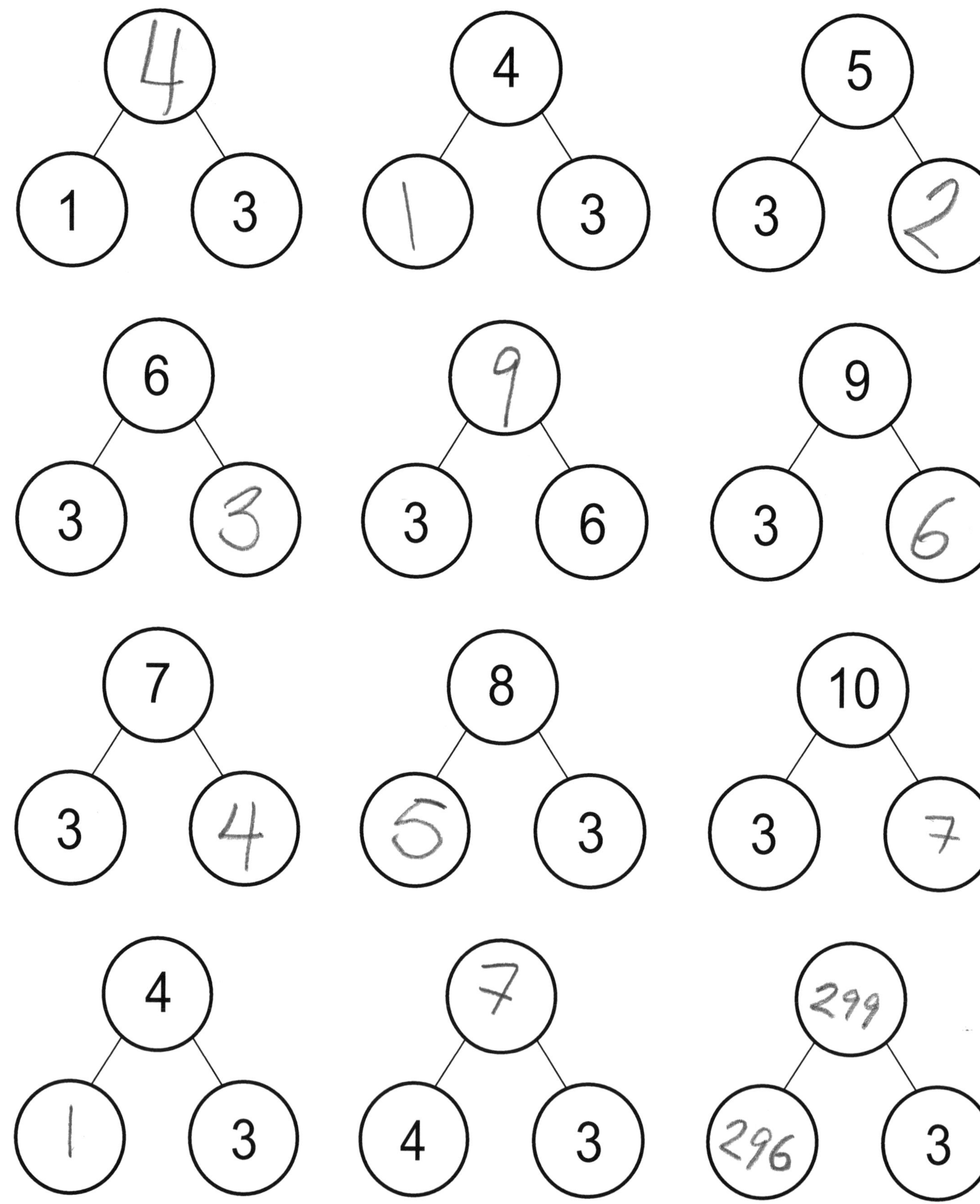

Complete the math sentences: Adding 3

$3 + 1 = \square$

$3 + \square = 3$

$\square + 3 = 4$

$2 + 3 = \square$

$3 + \square = 5$

$\square + 3 = 5$

$3 + 3 = \square$

$3 + \square = 7$

$\square + 3 = 8$

$3 + 4 = \square$

$3 + \square = 8$

$\square + 5 = 8$

$8 + 3 = \square$

$3 + 9 = \square$

Adding 4

1 + 4 = 5	2 + 4 = 6	3 + 4 = 7	4 + 4 = 8	5 + 4 = 9
6 + 4 = 10	7 + 4 = 11	8 + 4 = 12	9 + 4 = 13	10 + 4 = 14
4 + 1 = 5	4 + 2 = 6	4 + 3 = 7	4 + 4 = 8	4 + 5 = 9
4 + 6 = 10	4 + 7 = 11	4 + 8 = 12	4 + 9 = 13	4 + 10 = 14
4 + 5 = 9	4 + 8 = 12	4 + 2 = 6	7 + 4 = 11	9 + 4 = 13

Number Bonds: 4

Feb 9

Complete the math sentences: Adding 4

$4 + 1 = \square$

$4 + \square = 4$

$\square + 4 = 6$

$2 + 4 = \square$

$4 + \square = 5$

$\square + 4 = 7$

$3 + 4 = \square$

$4 + \square = 8$

$\square + 4 = 9$

$4 + 4 = \square$

$4 + \square = 10$

$\square + 3 = 7$

$8 + 4 = \square$

$4 + 9 = \square$

Feb 9

Adding 5

1 + 5	2 + 5	3 + 5	4 + 5	5 + 5
6 + 5	7 + 5	8 + 5	9 + 5	10 + 5
5 + 1	5 + 2	5 + 3	5 + 4	5 + 5
5 + 6	5 + 7	5 + 8	5 + 9	5 + 10
5 + 5	5 + 3	5 + 2	10 + 5	0 + 5

Number Bonds: 5

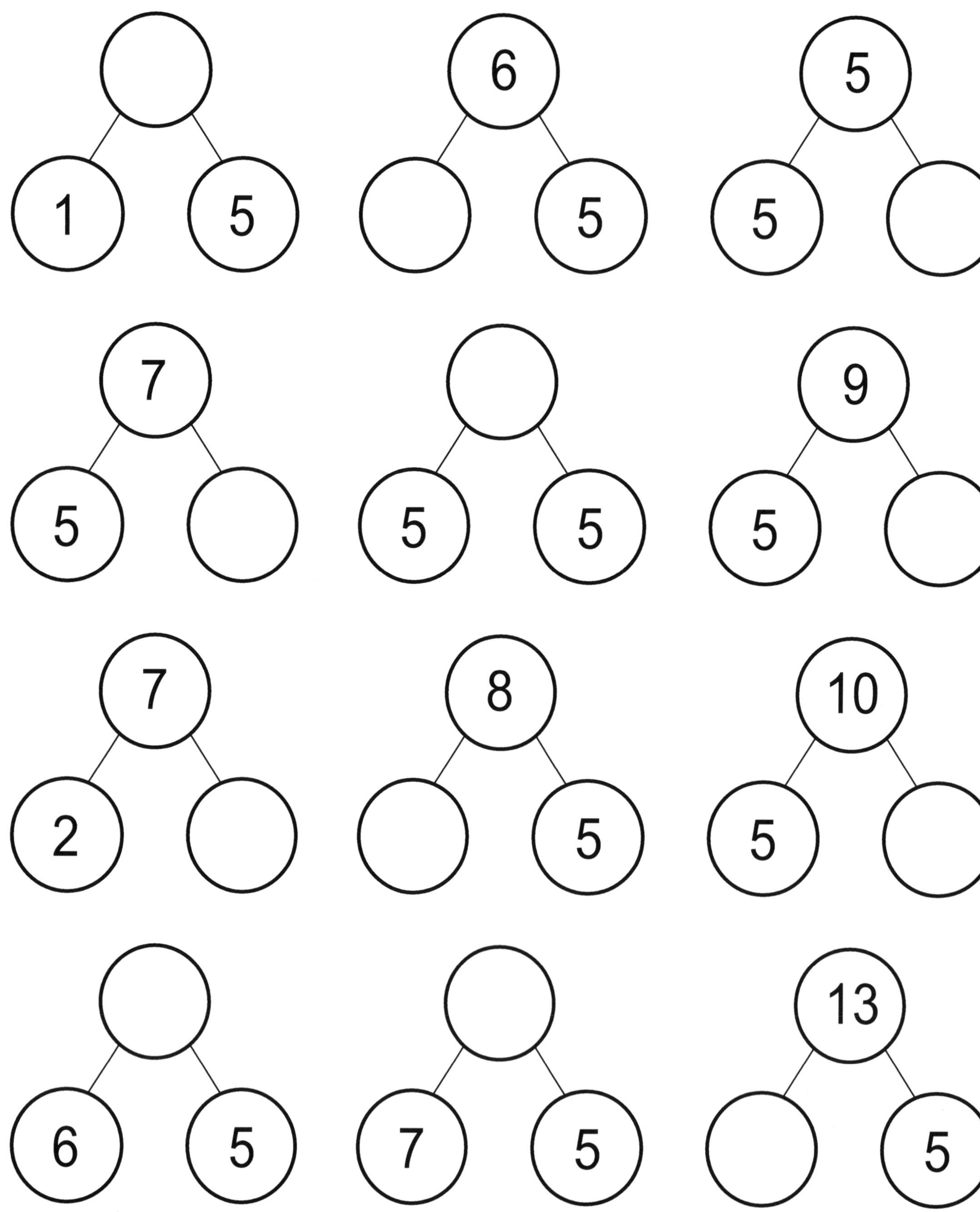

Complete the math sentences: Adding 5

$5 + 1 = \square$

$5 + \square = 5$

$\square + 5 = 6$

$2 + 5 = \square$

$5 + \square = 7$

$\square + 5 = 8$

$3 + 5 = \square$

$5 + \square = 9$

$\square + 5 = 10$

$4 + 5 = \square$

$5 + \square = 11$

$\square + 5 = 12$

$6 + 5 = \square$

$5 + 7 = \square$

Review: Adding 1 to 5

1	2	3	4	5
+ 5	+ 5	+ 5	+ 5	+ 5
2	1	3	4	4
+ 3	+ 4	+ 4	+ 5	+ 4
3	3	2	1	0
+ 3	+ 5	+ 1	+ 4	+ 5
5	3	3	1	2
+ 4	+ 2	+ 0	+ 3	+ 2
5	1	4	0	5
+ 5	+ 1	+ 4	+ 1	+ 2

Review: Number Bonds

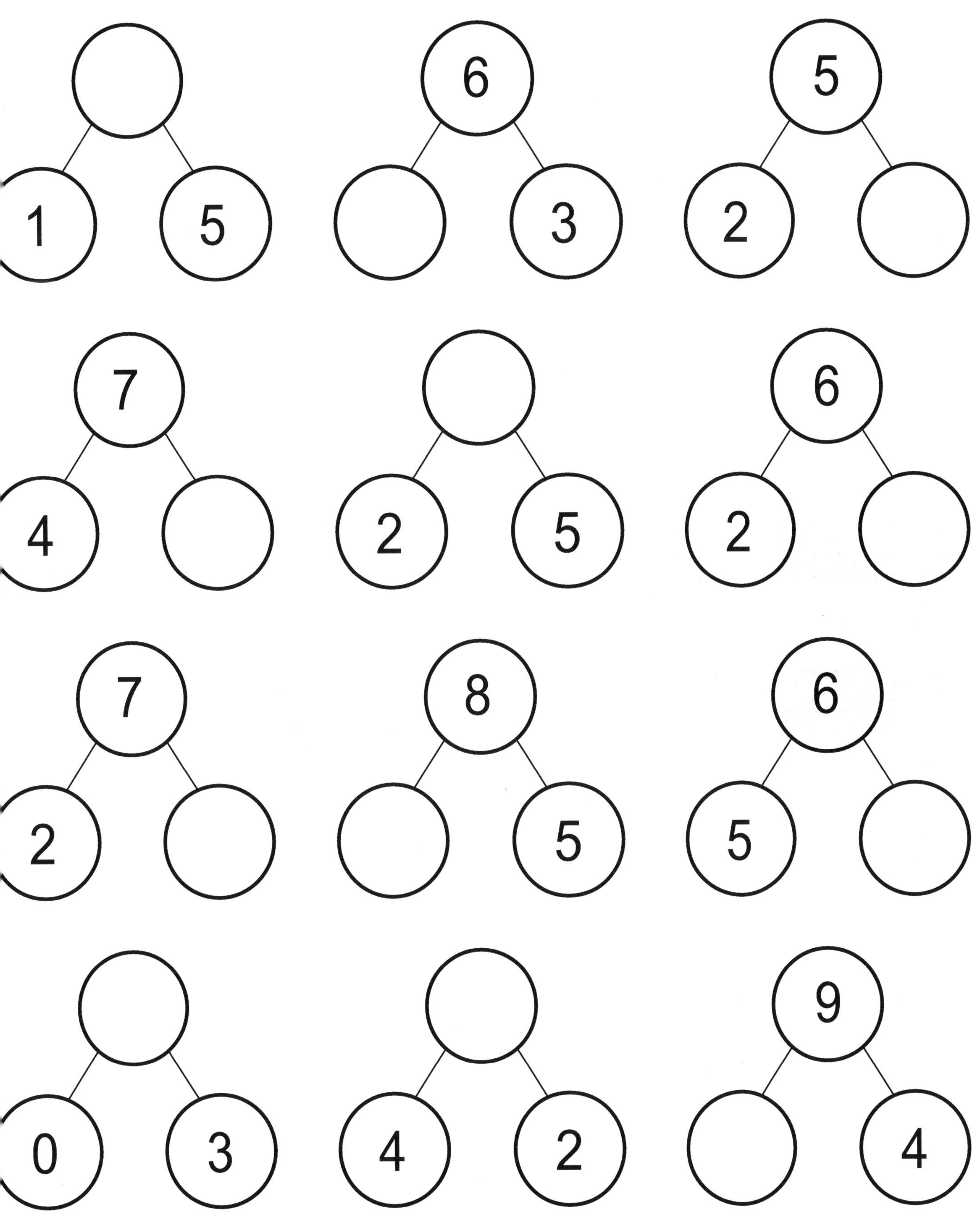

Review: Complete the math sentences 1 to 5

$1 + 1 = \square$

$3 + \square = 5$

$\square + 4 = 6$

$2 + 5 = \square$

$4 + \square = 7$

$\square + 5 = 8$

$3 + 1 = \square$

$4 + \square = 9$

$\square + 5 = 10$

$3 + 5 = \square$

$5 + \square = 9$

$\square + 5 = 8$

$2 + 1 = \square$

$5 + 2 = \square$

Number Bonds: Make 5

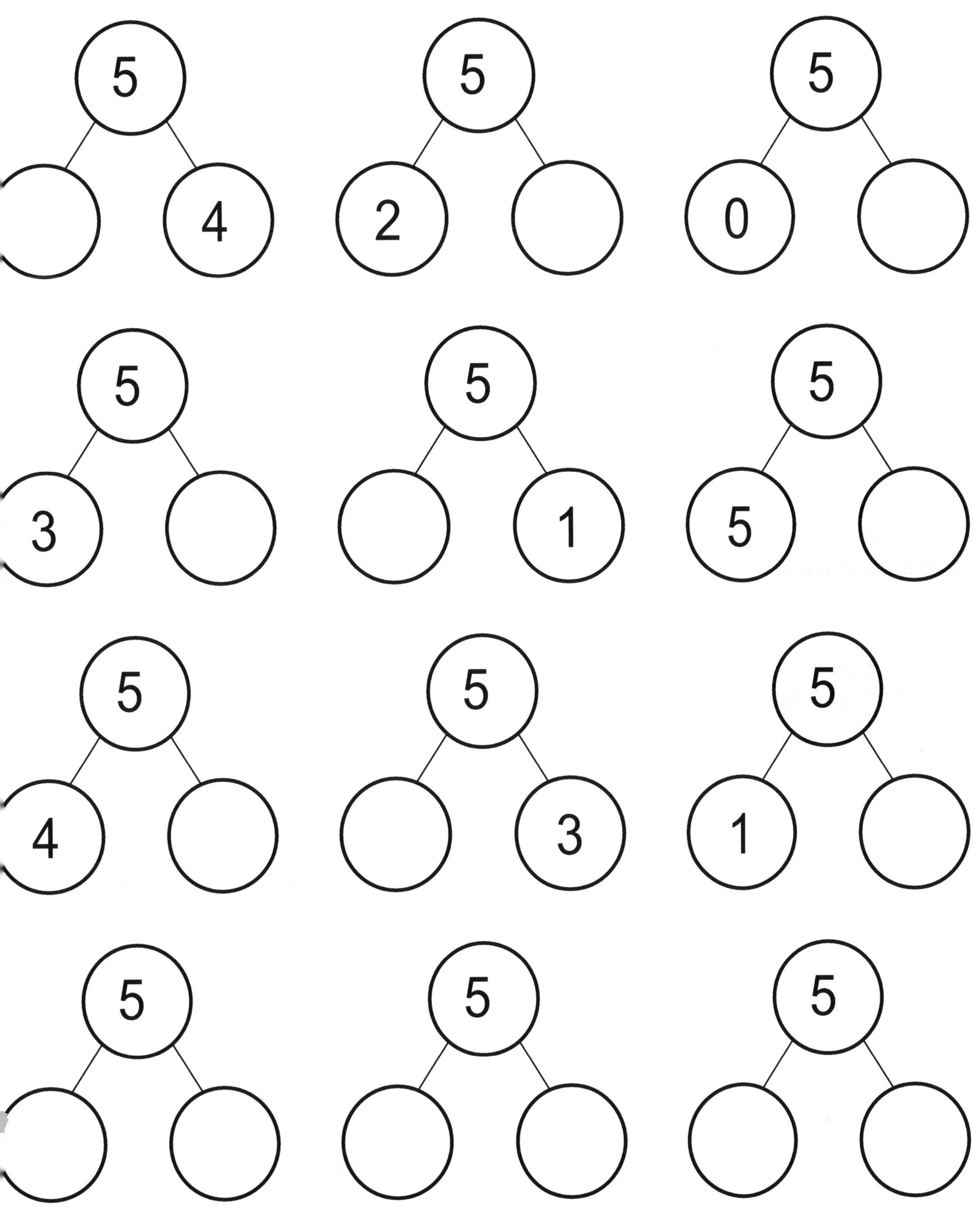

$$\begin{array}{r} 1 \\ +\ 6 \\ \hline \end{array} \qquad \begin{array}{r} 2 \\ +\ 6 \\ \hline \end{array} \qquad \begin{array}{r} 3 \\ +\ 6 \\ \hline \end{array} \qquad \begin{array}{r} 4 \\ +\ 6 \\ \hline \end{array} \qquad \begin{array}{r} 5 \\ +\ 6 \\ \hline \end{array}$$

$$\begin{array}{r} 6 \\ +\ 6 \\ \hline \end{array} \qquad \begin{array}{r} 7 \\ +\ 6 \\ \hline \end{array} \qquad \begin{array}{r} 8 \\ +\ 6 \\ \hline \end{array} \qquad \begin{array}{r} 9 \\ +\ 6 \\ \hline \end{array} \qquad \begin{array}{r} 10 \\ +\ 6 \\ \hline \end{array}$$

$$\begin{array}{r} 6 \\ +\ 1 \\ \hline \end{array} \qquad \begin{array}{r} 6 \\ +\ 2 \\ \hline \end{array} \qquad \begin{array}{r} 6 \\ +\ 3 \\ \hline \end{array} \qquad \begin{array}{r} 6 \\ +\ 4 \\ \hline \end{array} \qquad \begin{array}{r} 6 \\ +\ 5 \\ \hline \end{array}$$

$$\begin{array}{r} 0 \\ +\ 6 \\ \hline \end{array} \qquad \begin{array}{r} 4 \\ +\ 6 \\ \hline \end{array} \qquad \begin{array}{r} 6 \\ +\ 0 \\ \hline \end{array} \qquad \begin{array}{r} 6 \\ +\ 10 \\ \hline \end{array} \qquad \begin{array}{r} 6 \\ +\ 9 \\ \hline \end{array}$$

$$\begin{array}{r} 6 \\ +\ 3 \\ \hline \end{array} \qquad \begin{array}{r} 2 \\ +\ 6 \\ \hline \end{array} \qquad \begin{array}{r} 6 \\ +\ 4 \\ \hline \end{array} \qquad \begin{array}{r} 10 \\ +\ 6 \\ \hline \end{array} \qquad \begin{array}{r} 9 \\ +\ 6 \\ \hline \end{array}$$

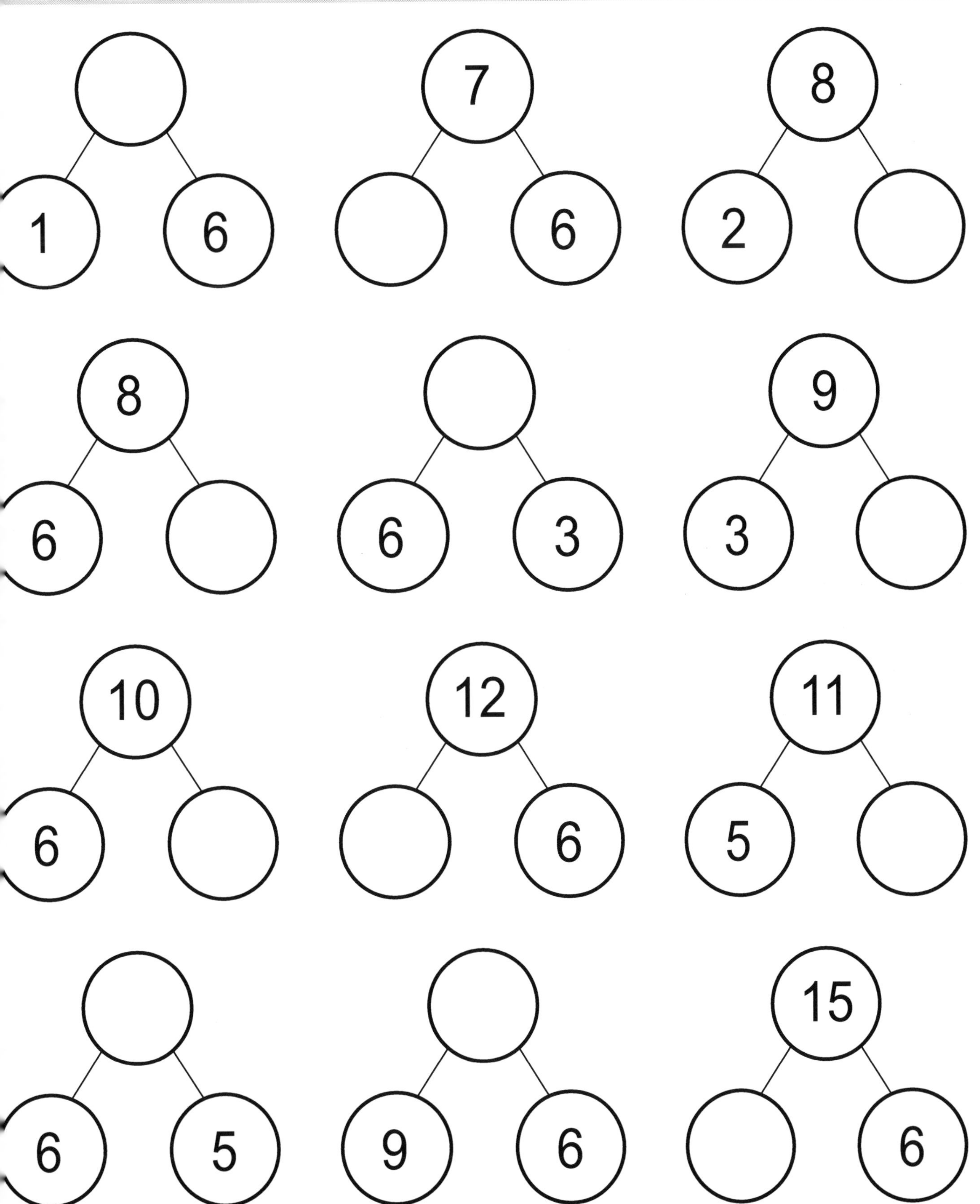
1
6
7
6
8
2
8
6
6
3
9
3
10
6
12
6
11
5
6
5
9
6
15
6

6 + 1 = ☐

6 + ☐ = 6

☐ + 6 = 7

2 + 6 = ☐

6 + ☐ = 8

☐ + 6 = 9

3 + 6 = ☐

6 + ☐ = 10

☐ + 5 = 11

4 + 6 = ☐

6 + ☐ = 12

☐ + 6 = 13

6 + 7 = ☐

6 + 9 = ☐

$1 + 7$	$2 + 7$	$3 + 7$	$4 + 7$	$5 + 7$
$6 + 7$	$7 + 7$	$8 + 7$	$9 + 7$	$10 + 7$
$7 + 1$	$7 + 2$	$7 + 3$	$7 + 4$	$7 + 5$
$0 + 7$	$3 + 7$	$7 + 2$	$7 + 10$	$7 + 9$
$7 + 3$	$2 + 7$	$7 + 4$	$10 + 7$	$9 + 7$

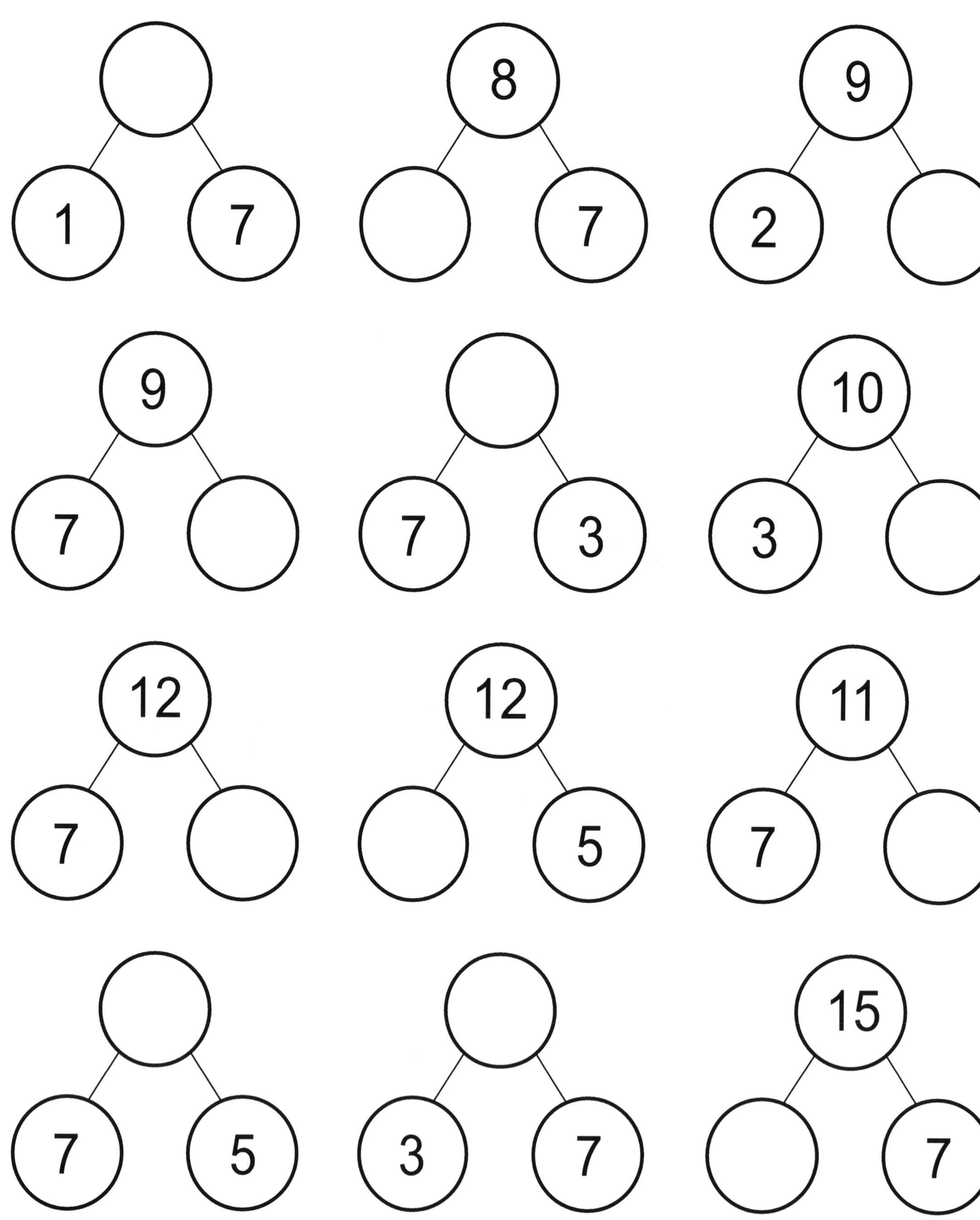
1
7
8
7
9
2
9
7
7
3
10
3
12
7
12
5
11
7
7
5
3
7
15
7

7 + 1 = ☐

7 + ☐ = 7

☐ + 7 = 8

2 + 7 = ☐

7 + ☐ = 9

☐ + 7 = 10

3 + 7 = ☐

3 + ☐ = 10

☐ + 7 = 11

4 + 7 = ☐

7 + ☐ = 12

☐ + 7 = 13

5 + 7 = ☐

7 + 8 = ☐

1 + 8	2 + 8	3 + 8	4 + 8	5 + 8
6 + 8	7 + 8	8 + 8	9 + 8	10 + 8
8 + 1	8 + 2	8 + 3	8 + 4	8 + 5
0 + 8	3 + 8	8 + 2	8 + 10	8 + 7
8 + 3	2 + 8	8 + 4	10 + 8	9 + 8

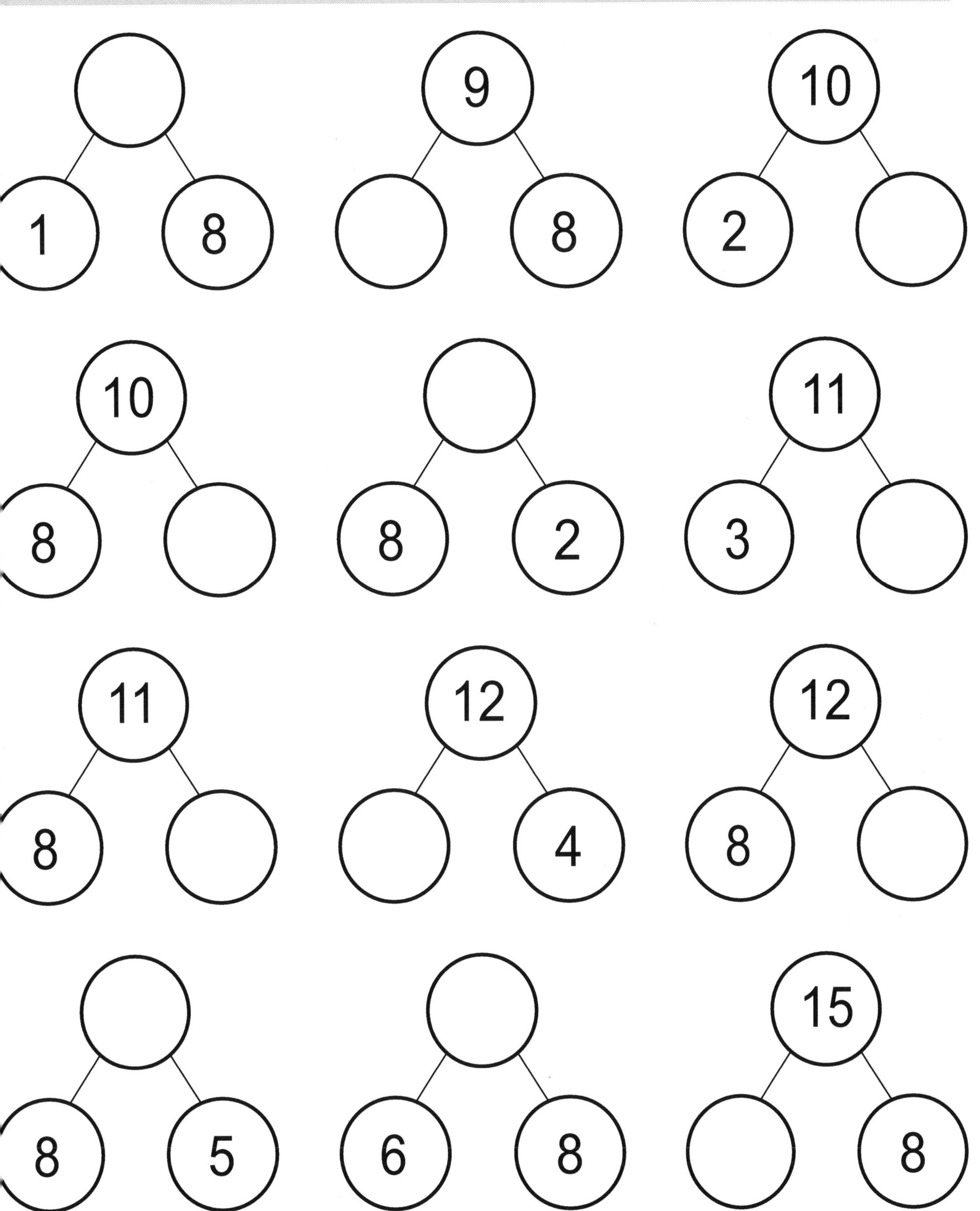
1
8
9
8
10
2
10
8
8
2
11
3
11
8
12
4
12
8
8
5
6
8
15
8

$8 + 1 = \square$

$8 + \square = 8$

$\square + 8 = 9$

$2 + 8 = \square$

$8 + \square = 10$

$\square + 2 = 10$

$3 + 8 = \square$

$3 + \square = 11$

$\square + 8 = 11$

$4 + 8 = \square$

$8 + \square = 12$

$\square + 8 = 13$

$6 + 8 = \square$

$7 + 8 = \square$

$\begin{array}{r} 1 \\ +\ 9 \\ \hline \end{array}$	$\begin{array}{r} 2 \\ +\ 9 \\ \hline \end{array}$	$\begin{array}{r} 3 \\ +\ 9 \\ \hline \end{array}$	$\begin{array}{r} 4 \\ +\ 9 \\ \hline \end{array}$	$\begin{array}{r} 5 \\ +\ 9 \\ \hline \end{array}$
$\begin{array}{r} 6 \\ +\ 9 \\ \hline \end{array}$	$\begin{array}{r} 7 \\ +\ 9 \\ \hline \end{array}$	$\begin{array}{r} 8 \\ +\ 9 \\ \hline \end{array}$	$\begin{array}{r} 9 \\ +\ 9 \\ \hline \end{array}$	$\begin{array}{r} 10 \\ +\ 9 \\ \hline \end{array}$
$\begin{array}{r} 9 \\ +\ 1 \\ \hline \end{array}$	$\begin{array}{r} 9 \\ +\ 2 \\ \hline \end{array}$	$\begin{array}{r} 9 \\ +\ 3 \\ \hline \end{array}$	$\begin{array}{r} 9 \\ +\ 4 \\ \hline \end{array}$	$\begin{array}{r} 9 \\ +\ 5 \\ \hline \end{array}$
$\begin{array}{r} 0 \\ +\ 9 \\ \hline \end{array}$	$\begin{array}{r} 3 \\ +\ 9 \\ \hline \end{array}$	$\begin{array}{r} 9 \\ +\ 2 \\ \hline \end{array}$	$\begin{array}{r} 9 \\ +\ 10 \\ \hline \end{array}$	$\begin{array}{r} 9 \\ +\ 6 \\ \hline \end{array}$
$\begin{array}{r} 9 \\ +\ 7 \\ \hline \end{array}$	$\begin{array}{r} 2 \\ +\ 9 \\ \hline \end{array}$	$\begin{array}{r} 9 \\ +\ 4 \\ \hline \end{array}$	$\begin{array}{r} 10 \\ +\ 9 \\ \hline \end{array}$	$\begin{array}{r} 11 \\ +\ 9 \\ \hline \end{array}$

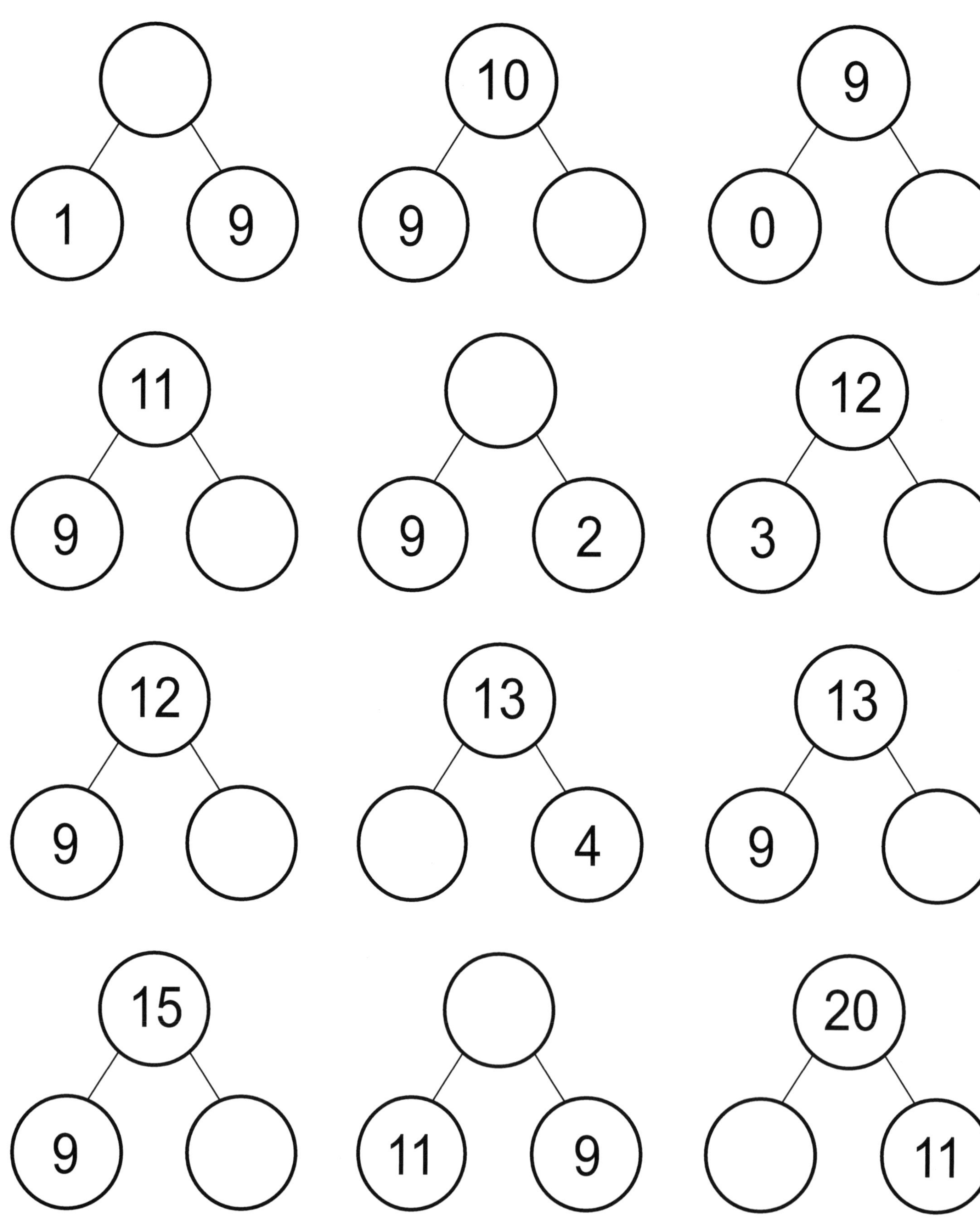
10
9
1
9
9
0
11
9
9
2
12
3
12
9
13
4
13
9
15
9
11
9
20
11

$9 + 1 = \square$

$9 + \square = 10$

$\square + 9 = 10$

$2 + 9 = \square$

$9 + \square = 11$

$\square + 2 = 11$

$3 + 9 = \square$

$3 + \square = 12$

$\square + 9 = 13$

$5 + 9 = \square$

$9 + \square = 15$

$\square + 6 = 15$

$9 + 10 = \square$

$11 + 9 = \square$

Adding 10

1	2	3	4	5
+ 10	+ 10	+ 10	+ 10	+ 10
6	7	8	9	10
+ 10	+ 10	+ 10	+ 10	+ 10
10	10	10	10	10
+ 1	+ 2	+ 3	+ 4	+ 5
0	3	10	10	10
+ 10	+ 10	+ 2	+ 10	+ 6
10	2	10	10	11
+ 7	+ 10	+ 4	+ 10	+ 10

Number Bonds: 10

Complete the math sentences: Adding 10

$10 + 1 = \square$

$10 + \square = 11$

$\square + 10 = 12$

$2 + 10 = \square$

$10 + \square = 13$

$\square + 3 = 13$

$4 + 10 = \square$

$4 + \square = 14$

$\square + 10 = 15$

$5 + 10 = \square$

$10 + \square = 17$

$\square + 6 = 16$

$8 + 10 = \square$

$10 + 9 = \square$

Review: Adding 1 to 10

2 + 3	4 + 5	6 + 4	3 + 7	8 + 2
5 + 5	6 + 5	7 + 2	9 + 1	4 + 7
10 + 1	7 + 5	2 + 10	2 + 4	3 + 5
4 + 8	6 + 9	10 + 5	10 + 10	7 + 6
8 + 7	9 + 10	8 + 5	9 + 7	2 + 9

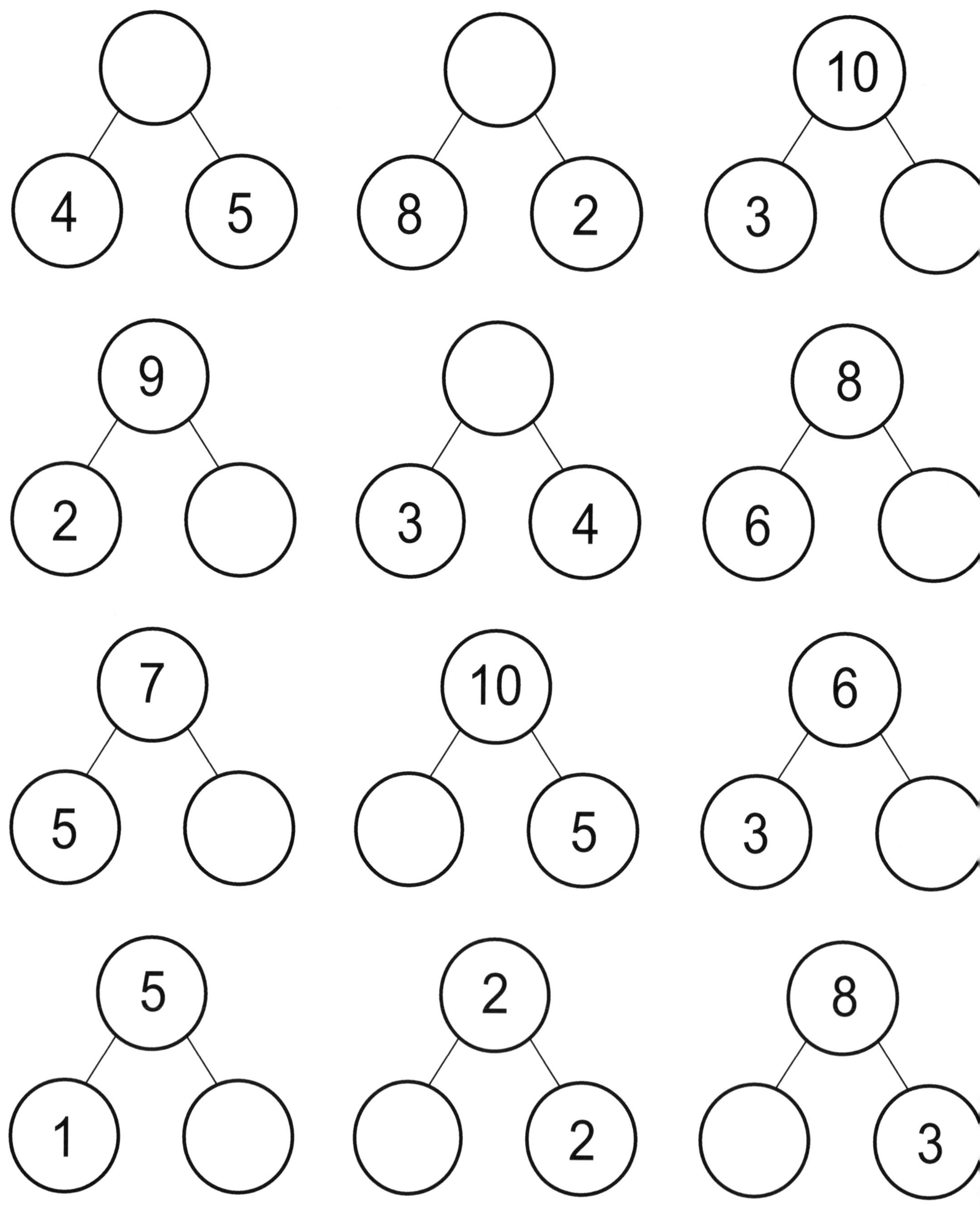
4
5
8
2
10
3
9
2
3
4
8
6
7
5
10
5
6
3
5
1
2
2
8
3

Review: Complete the math sentences

$10 + 3 = \square$

$2 + \square = 9$

$\square + 7 = 10$

$2 + 4 = \square$

$5 + \square = 12$

$\square + 3 = 9$

$4 + 3 = \square$

$4 + \square = 8$

$\square + 8 = 10$

$5 + 5 = \square$

$10 + \square = 17$

$\square + 2 = 7$

$8 + 3 = \square$

$7 + 9 = \square$

Number Bonds: Make 10

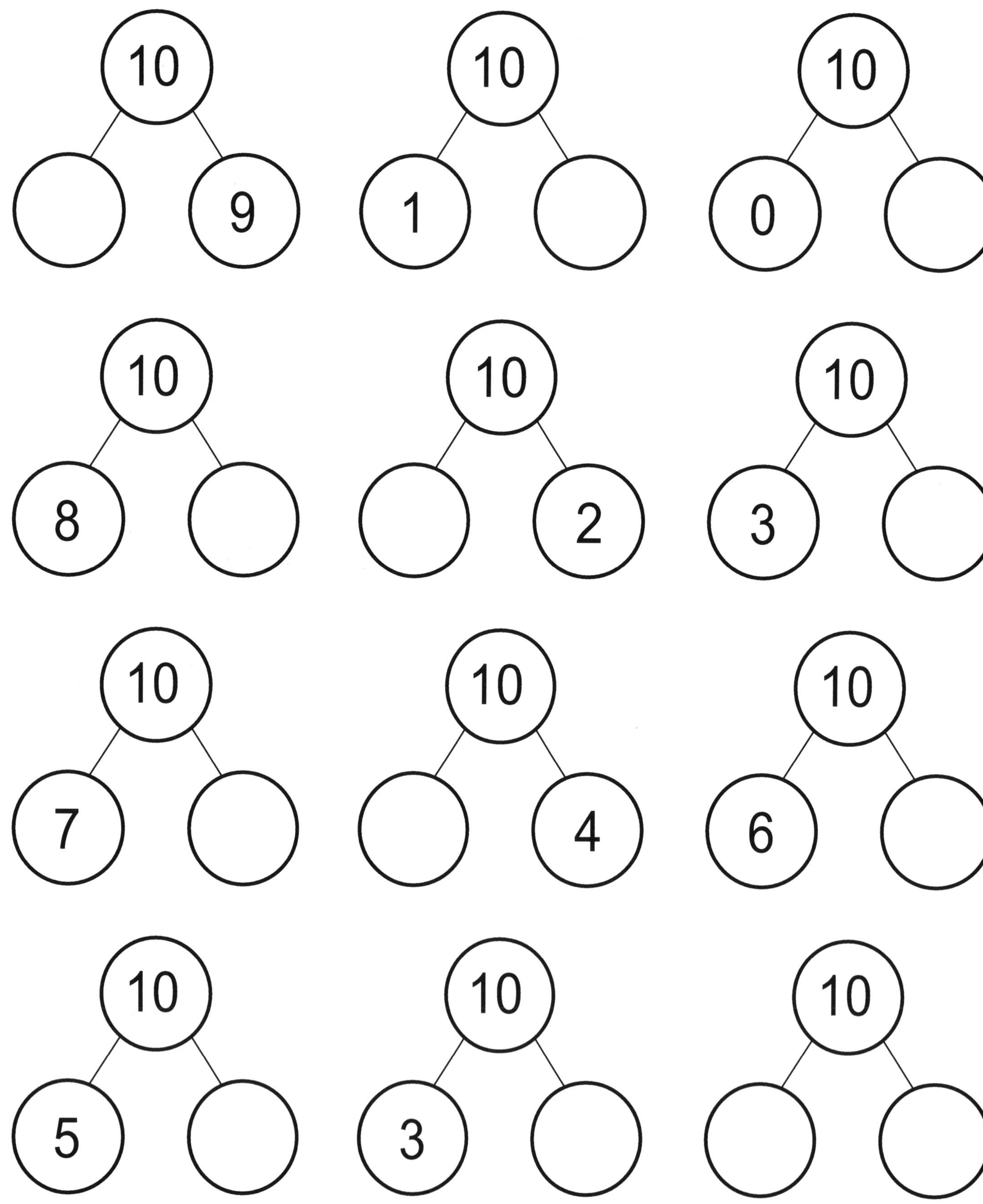

Challenge: Complete the number bond pyramid

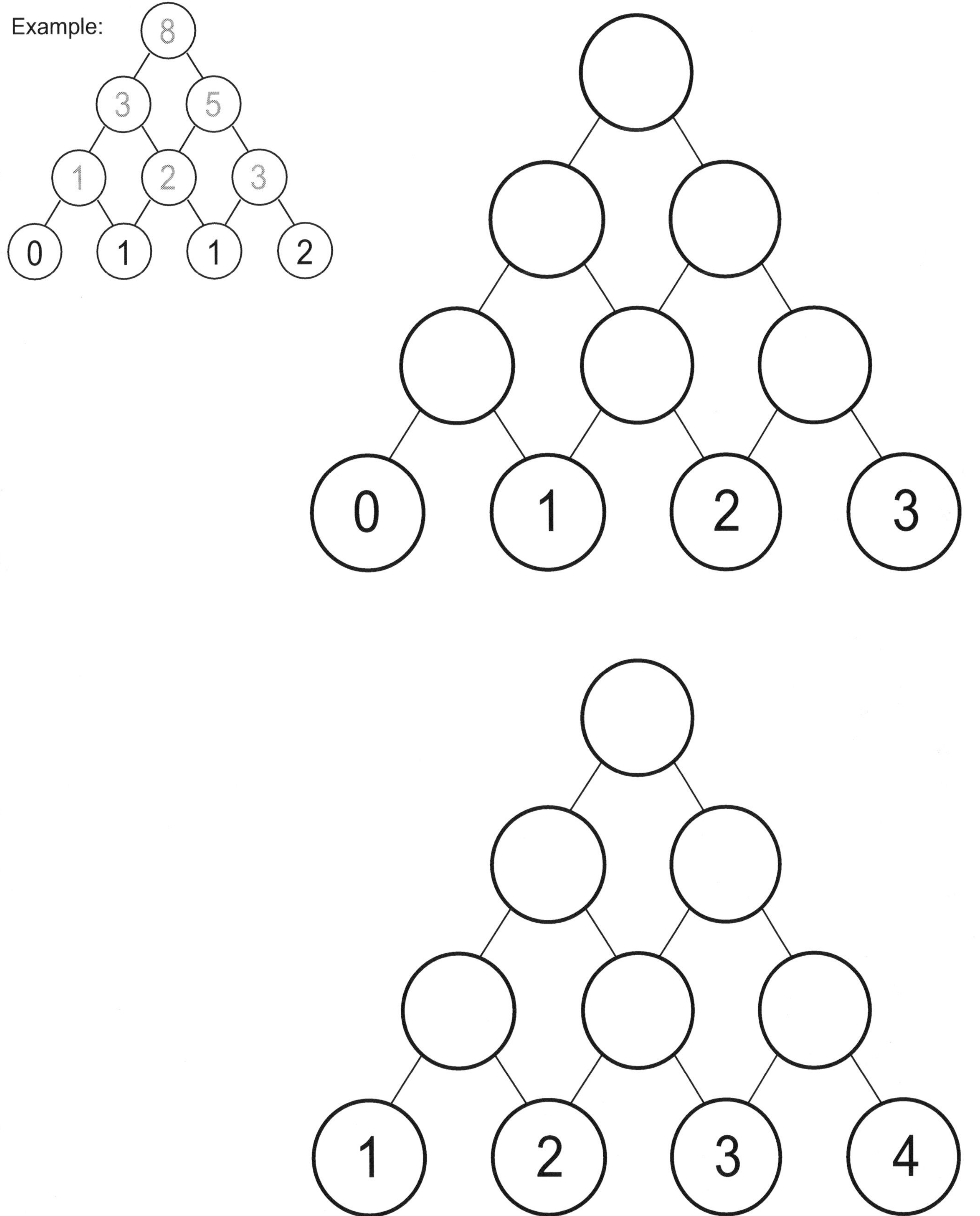

Number Bonds: Make 20

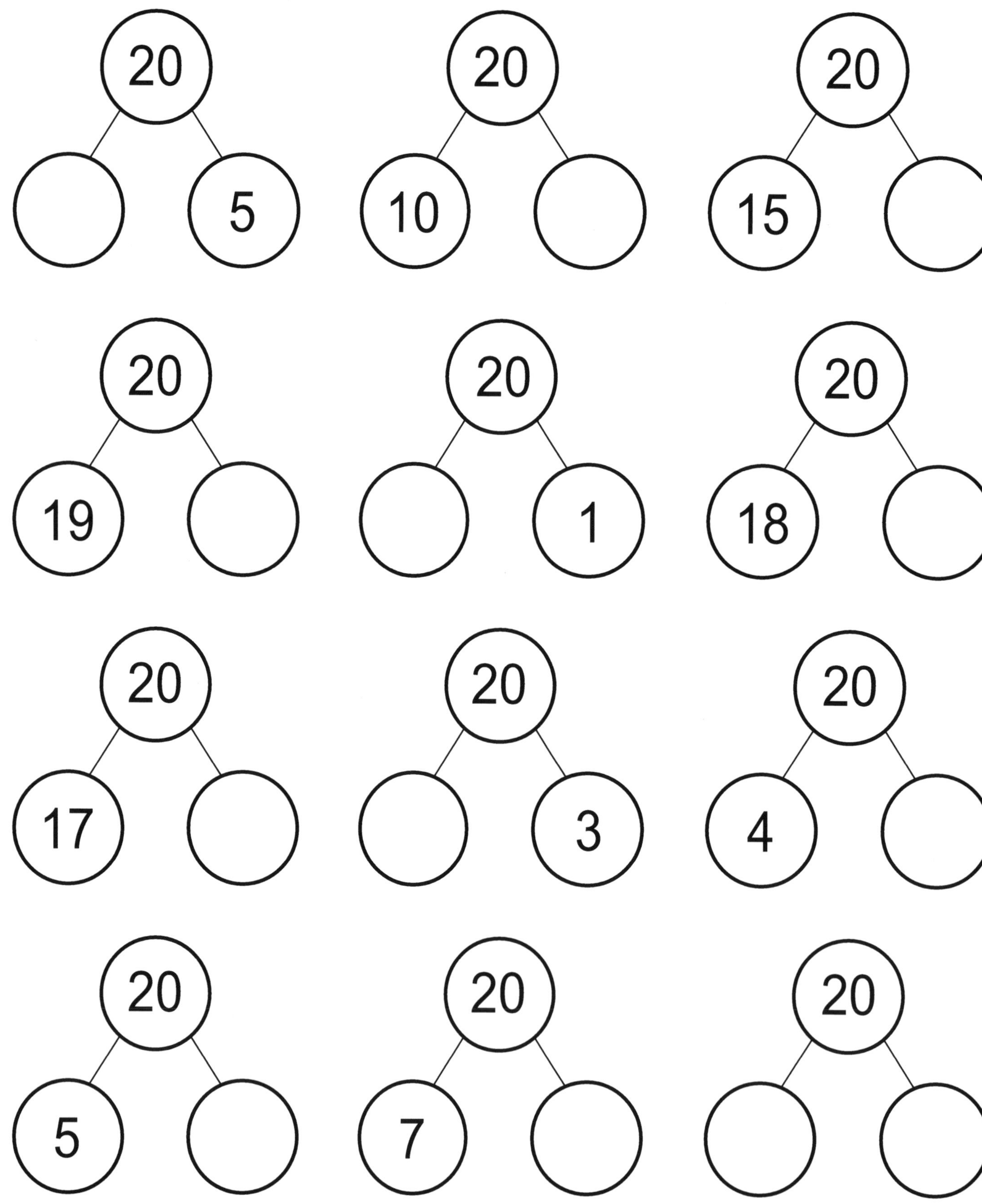

Subtracting 1

1 - 1	2 - 1	3 - 1	4 - 1	5 - 1
6 - 1	7 - 1	8 - 1	9 - 1	10 - 1
11 - 1	12 - 1	13 - 1	14 - 1	15 - 1
16 - 1	17 - 1	18 - 1	19 - 1	20 - 1
5 - 1	10 - 1	21 - 1	1 - 1	11 - 1

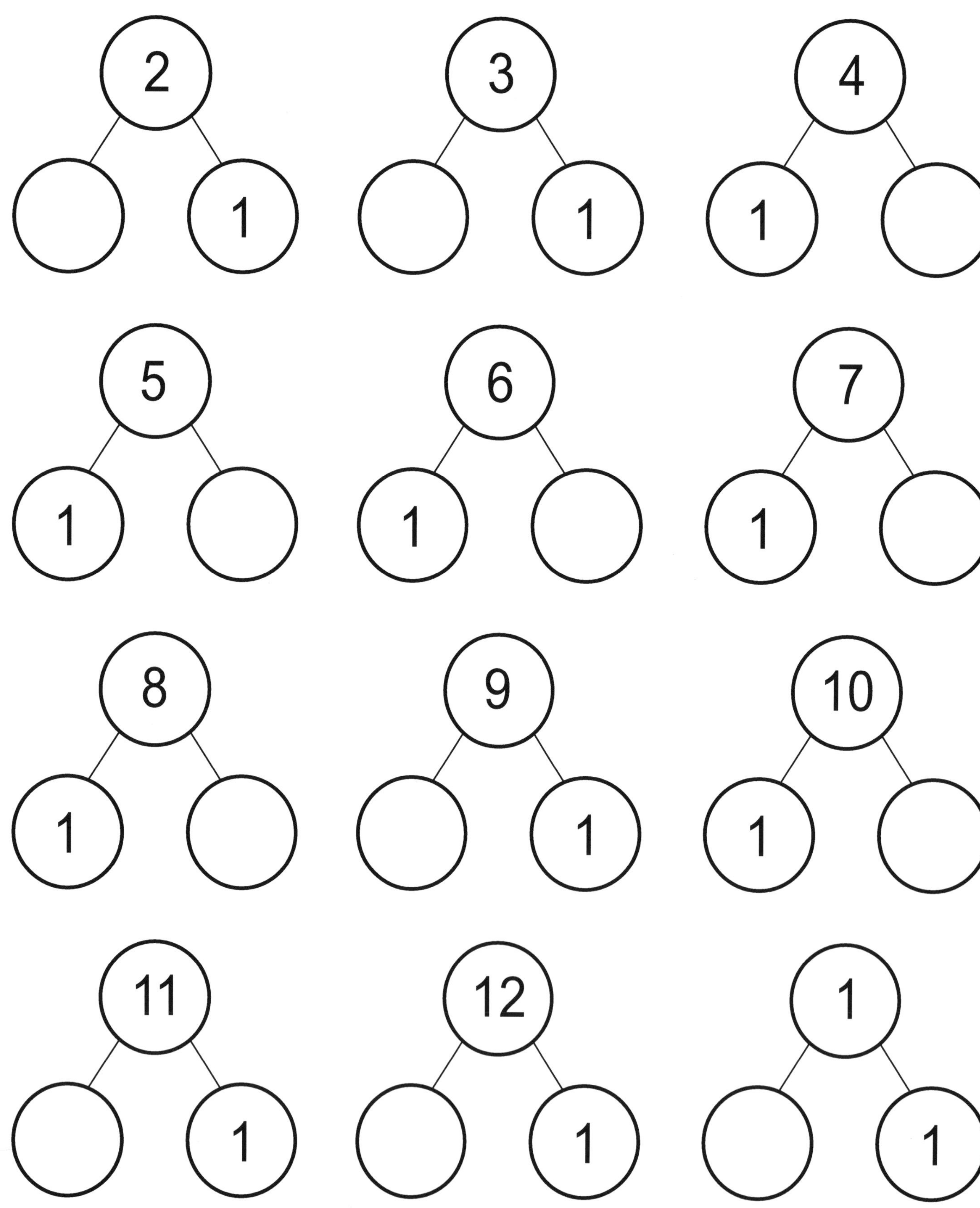
2
1
3
1
4
1
5
1
6
1
7
1
8
1
9
1
10
1
11
1
12
1
1
1

Complete the math sentences: Subtracting 1

1 - 1 = ☐

3 - ☐ = 2

☐ - 1 = 3

2 - 1 = ☐

5 - ☐ = 4

☐ - 1 = 3

3 - 1 = ☐

7 - ☐ = 6

☐ - 1 = 5

4 - 1 = ☐

8 - ☐ = 7

☐ - 1 = 6

9 - 1 = ☐

10 - 1 = ☐

Subtracting 2

3 - 2	2 - 2	3 - 2	4 - 2	5 - 2
6 - 2	7 - 2	8 - 2	9 - 2	10 - 2
11 - 2	12 - 2	13 - 2	14 - 2	15 - 2
16 - 2	17 - 2	18 - 2	19 - 2	20 - 2
5 - 2	10 - 2	15 - 2	20 - 2	12 - 2

Number Bonds: Subtracting 2

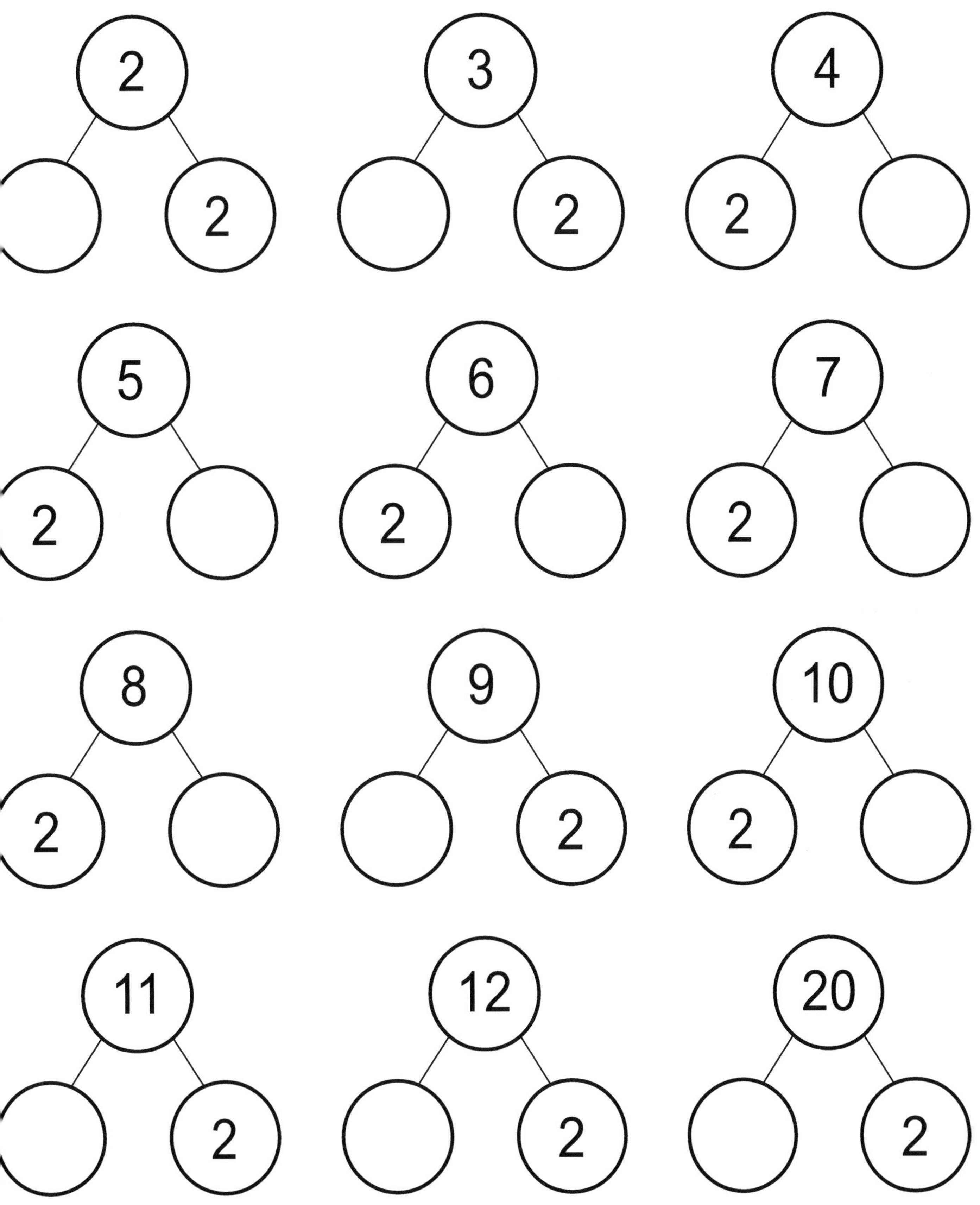

Complete the math sentences: Subtracting 2

2 - 2 = □

3 - □ = 1

□ - 2 = 2

5 - 2 = □

5 - □ = 3

□ - 2 = 3

4 - 2 = □

6 - □ = 4

□ - 2 = 5

7 - 2 = □

8 - □ = 6

□ - 2 = 7

9 - 2 = □

10 - 2 = □

Subtracting 3

3	4	5	6	7
- 3	- 3	- 3	- 3	- 3
6	7	8	9	10
- 3	- 3	- 3	- 3	- 3
11	12	13	14	15
- 3	- 3	- 3	- 3	- 3
16	17	18	19	20
- 3	- 3	- 3	- 3	- 3
5	10	15	20	13
- 3	- 3	- 3	- 3	- 3

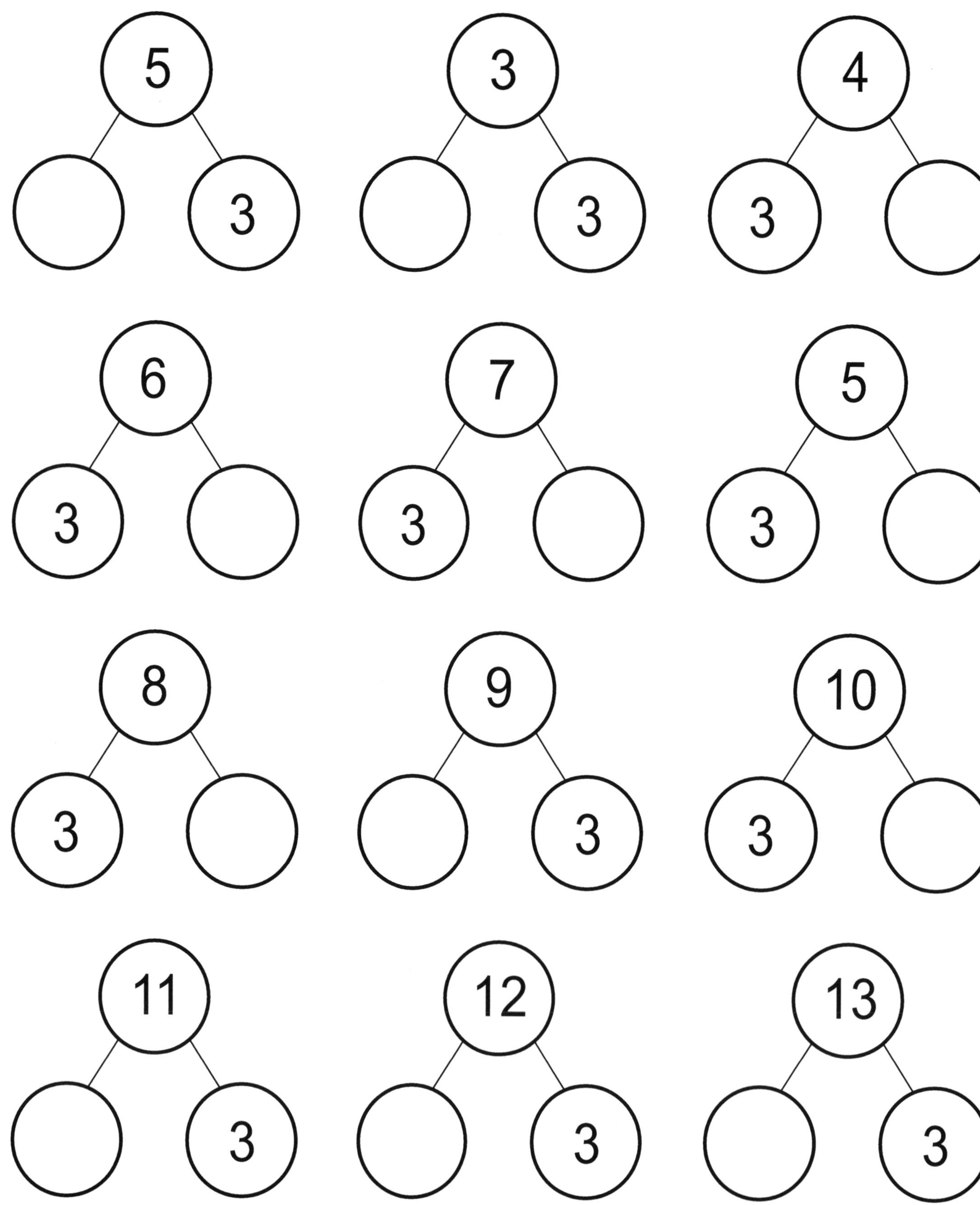
5
3
3
3
4
3
6
3
7
3
5
3
8
3
9
3
10
3
11
3
12
3
13
3

Complete the math sentences: Subtracting 3

4 - 3 = □

3 - □ = 0

□ - 3 = 2

5 - 3 = □

6 - □ = 3

□ - 3 = 4

7 - 3 = □

8 - □ = 5

□ - 3 = 5

9 - 3 = □

9 - □ = 6

□ - 3 = 7

9 - 3 = □

10 - 3 = □

Subtracting 4

5 - 4 = ___	4 - 4 = ___	5 - 4 = ___	6 - 4 = ___	7 - 4 = ___
6 - 4 = ___	7 - 4 = ___	8 - 4 = ___	9 - 4 = ___	10 - 4 = ___
11 - 4 = ___	12 - 4 = ___	13 - 4 = ___	14 - 4 = ___	15 - 4 = ___
16 - 4 = ___	17 - 4 = ___	18 - 4 = ___	19 - 4 = ___	20 - 4 = ___
5 - 4 = ___	10 - 4 = ___	15 - 4 = ___	20 - 4 = ___	14 - 4 = ___

Number Bonds: Subtracting 4

Complete the math sentences: Subtracting 4

$4 - 4 = \square$

$4 - \square = 0$

$\square - 4 = 2$

$6 - 4 = \square$

$7 - \square = 3$

$\square - 4 = 4$

$8 - 4 = \square$

$9 - \square = 5$

$\square - 4 = 5$

$10 - 4 = \square$

$10 - \square = 6$

$\square - 4 = 7$

$11 - 4 = \square$

$10 - 4 = \square$

Subtracting 5

6	10	5	6	7
- 5	- 5	- 5	- 5	- 5
6	7	8	9	10
- 5	- 5	- 5	- 5	- 5
11	12	13	14	15
- 5	- 5	- 5	- 5	- 5
16	17	18	19	20
- 5	- 5	- 5	- 5	- 5
5	10	15	20	25
- 5	- 5	- 5	- 5	- 5

Number Bonds: Subtracting 5

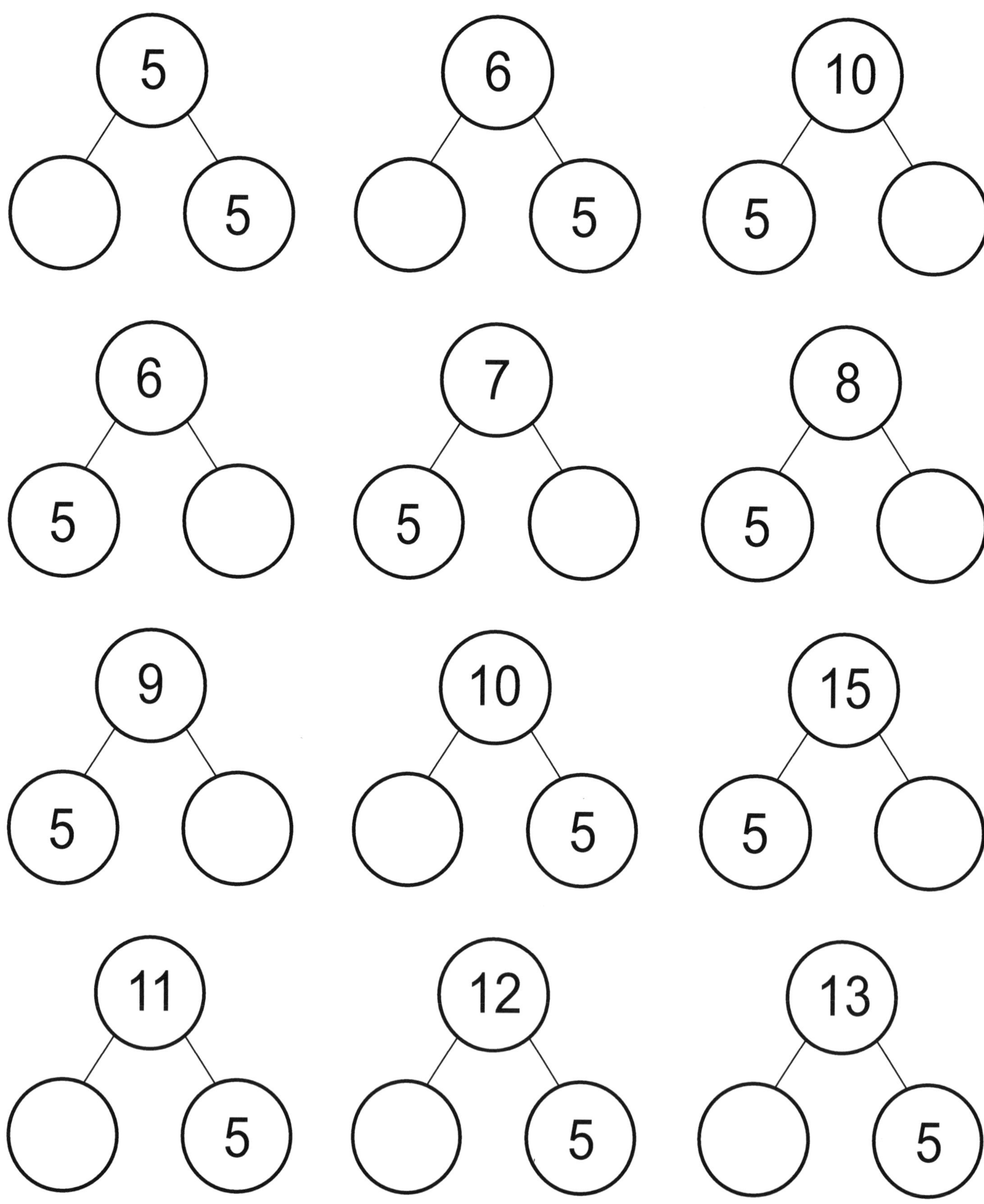

Complete the math sentences -- Subtracting 5

$5 - 5 = \square$

$5 - \square = 0$

$\square - 5 = 1$

$6 - 5 = \square$

$7 - \square = 2$

$\square - 5 = 3$

$8 - 5 = \square$

$9 - \square = 4$

$\square - 5 = 5$

$10 - 5 = \square$

$11 - \square = 6$

$\square - 5 = 7$

$15 - 5 = \square$

$20 - 5 = \square$

Review: Subtracting 1 to 5

6 - 5	10 - 4	5 - 3	6 - 2	7 - 4
6 - 1	7 - 3	8 - 4	9 - 2	10 - 5
11 - 5	10 - 4	13 - 3	10 - 2	15 - 5
9 - 4	9 - 3	5 - 2	7 - 4	8 - 5
9 - 2	4 - 3	8 - 2	6 - 4	7 - 5

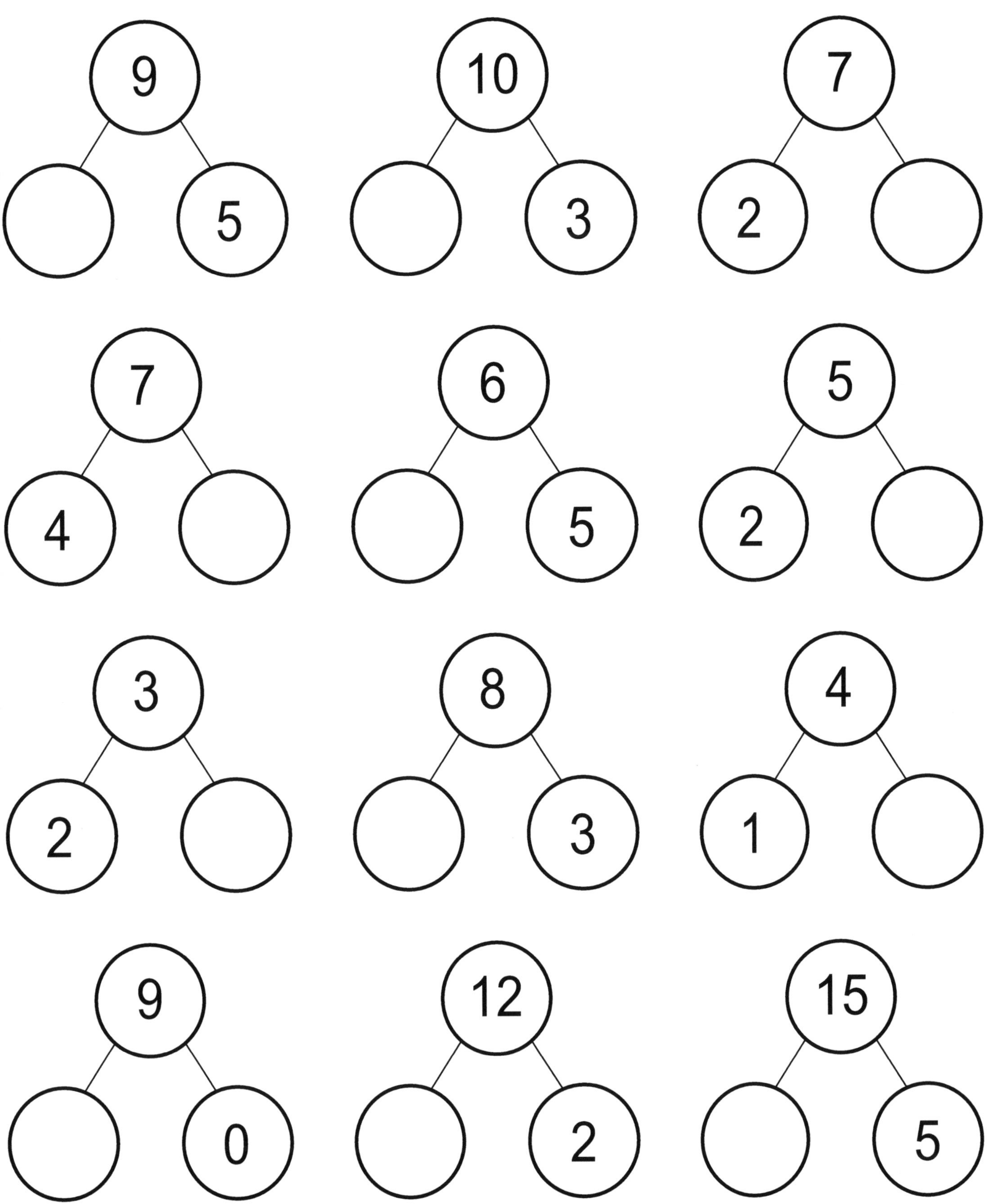
9
5
10
3
7
2
7
4
6
5
5
2
3
2
8
3
4
1
9
0
12
2
15
5

Review: Complete the math sentences

$5 - 5 = \square$

$8 - \square = 4$

$\square - 3 = 1$

$6 - 4 = \square$

$7 - \square = 2$

$\square - 4 = 3$

$9 - 5 = \square$

$9 - \square = 3$

$\square - 4 = 3$

$10 - 4 = \square$

$9 - \square = 6$

$\square - 3 = 7$

$7 - 5 = \square$

$8 - 5 = \square$

Subtracting 6

6 - 6	10 - 6	8 - 6	9 - 6	7 - 6
10 - 6	7 - 6	8 - 6	11 - 6	12 - 6
11 - 6	12 - 6	13 - 6	14 - 6	15 - 6
16 - 6	17 - 6	18 - 6	19 - 6	20 - 6
8 - 6	10 - 6	15 - 6	16 - 6	20 - 6

Number Bonds: Subtracting 6

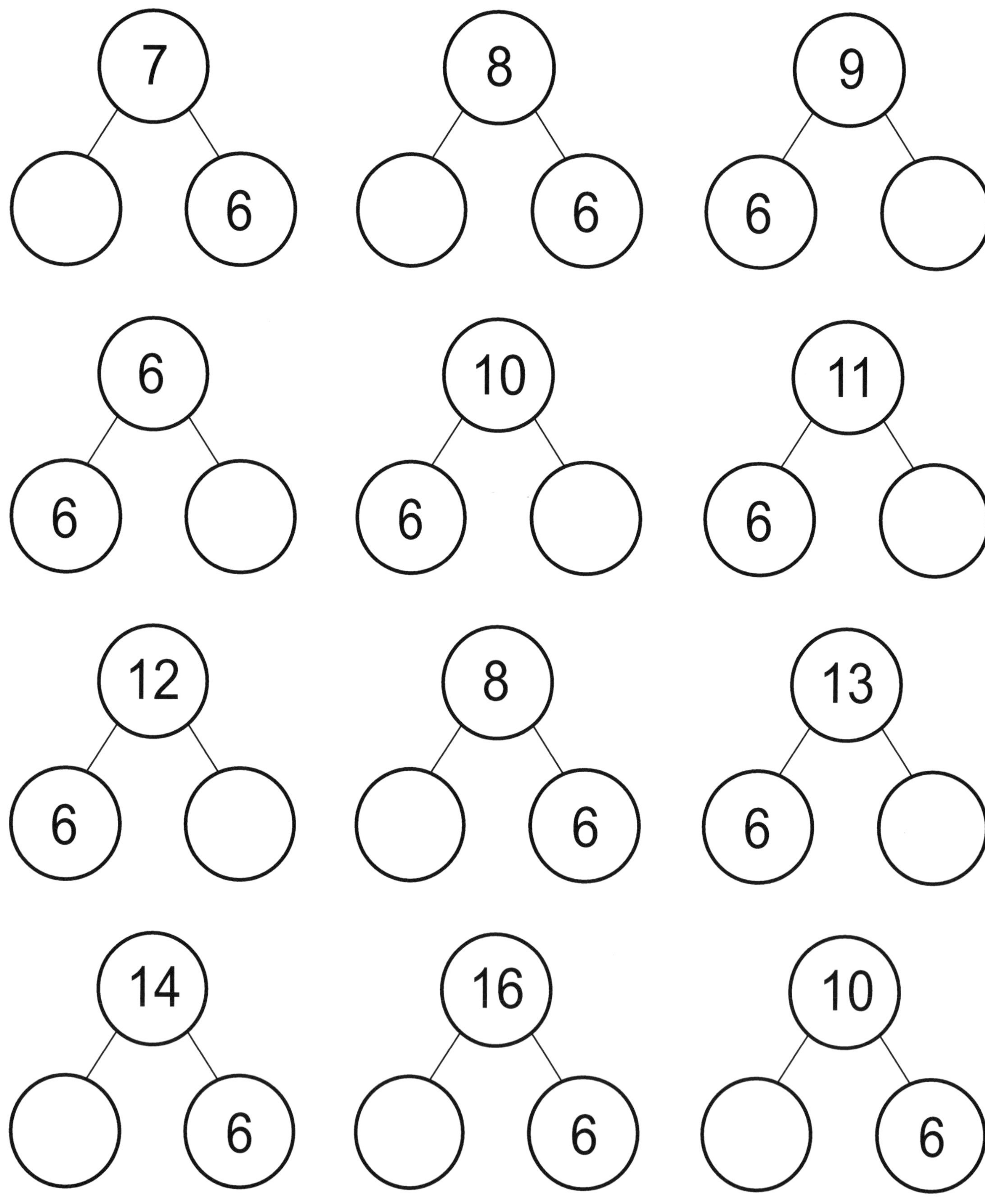

Complete the math sentences: Subtracting 6

$7 - 6 = \square$

$6 - \square = 0$

$\square - 6 = 1$

$8 - 6 = \square$

$8 - \square = 2$

$\square - 6 = 3$

$8 - 6 = \square$

$10 - \square = 4$

$\square - 6 = 4$

$11 - 6 = \square$

$11 - \square = 5$

$\square - 6 = 6$

$13 - 6 = \square$

$12 - 6 = \square$

Subtracting 7

7 - 7	10 - 7	8 - 7	9 - 7	12 - 7
9 - 7	7 - 7	8 - 7	10 - 7	17 - 7
11 - 7	12 - 7	13 - 7	14 - 7	15 - 7
16 - 7	17 - 7	18 - 7	19 - 7	20 - 7
8 - 7	10 - 7	14 - 7	15 - 7	20 - 7

Number Bonds: Subtracting 7

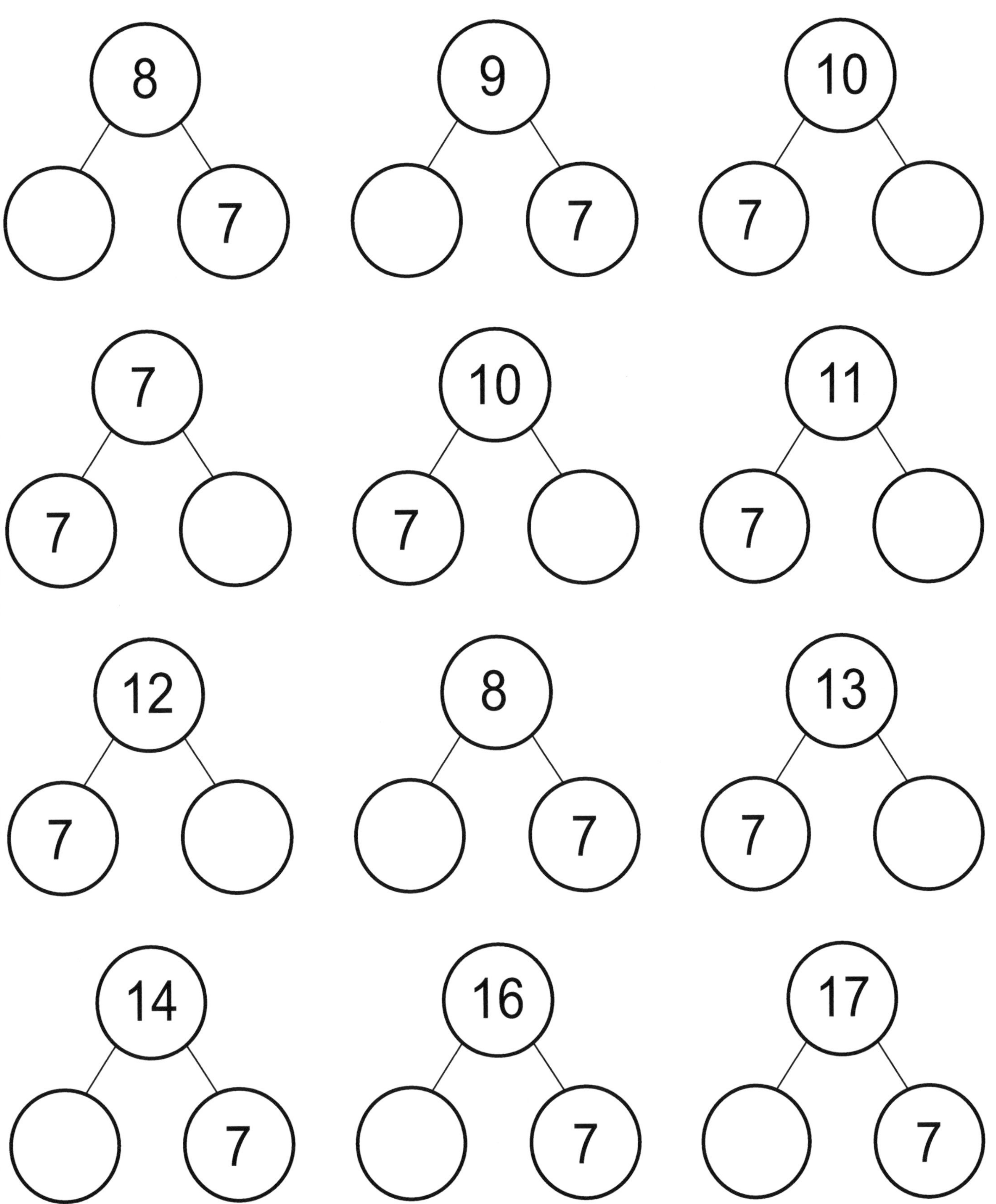

Complete the math sentences: Subtracting 7

$7 - 7 = \square$

$7 - \square = 0$

$\square - 7 = 1$

$8 - 7 = \square$

$9 - \square = 2$

$\square - 7 = 3$

$8 - 7 = \square$

$10 - \square = 3$

$\square - 7 = 4$

$11 - 7 = \square$

$14 - \square = 7$

$\square - 7 = 6$

$13 - 7 = \square$

$17 - 7 = \square$

Subtracting 8

9 − 8 = ___	10 − 8 = ___	8 − 8 = ___	9 − 8 = ___	12 − 8 = ___
9 − 8 = ___	11 − 8 = ___	18 − 8 = ___	10 − 8 = ___	20 − 8 = ___
11 − 8 = ___	12 − 8 = ___	13 − 8 = ___	14 − 8 = ___	15 − 8 = ___
16 − 8 = ___	17 − 8 = ___	18 − 8 = ___	19 − 8 = ___	20 − 8 = ___
8 − 8 = ___	10 − 8 = ___	12 − 8 = ___	16 − 8 = ___	18 − 8 = ___

Number Bonds: Subtracting 8

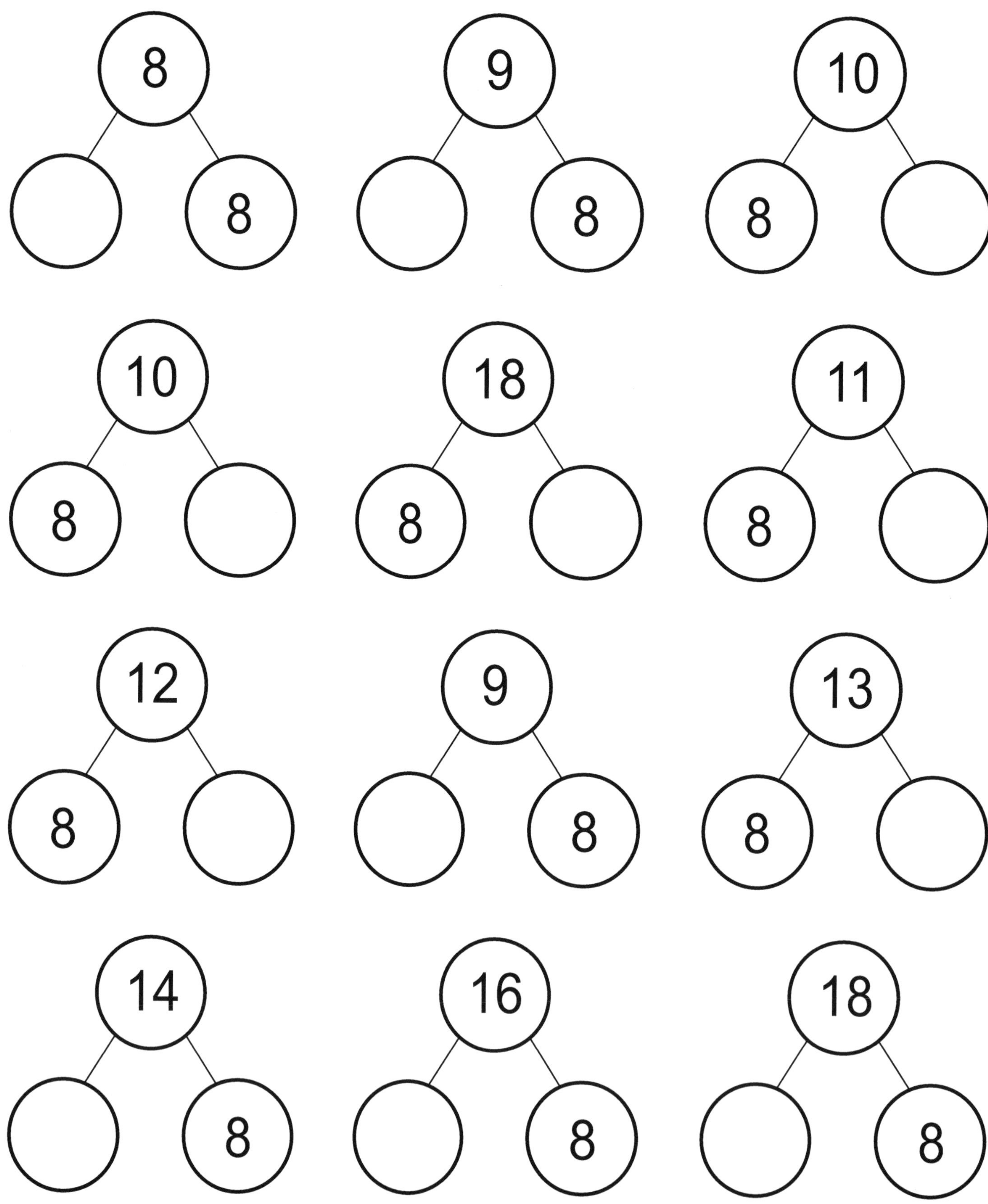

Complete the math sentences: Subtracting 8

8 - 8 = ☐	8 - ☐ = 0
☐ - 8 = 1	9 - 8 = ☐
10 - ☐ = 2	☐ - 8 = 3
12 - 8 = ☐	11 - ☐ = 3
☐ - 8 = 4	18 - 8 = ☐
15 - ☐ = 7	☐ - 8 = 6
13 - 8 = ☐	16 - 8 = ☐

Subtracting 9

9 - 9	10 - 9	11 - 9	19 - 9	20 - 9
12 - 9	13 - 9	14 - 9	15 - 9	16 - 9
17 - 9	18 - 9	19 - 9	20 - 9	10 - 9
11 - 9	19 - 9	20 - 9	30 - 9	40 - 9
9 - 9	10 - 9	12 - 9	16 - 9	18 - 9

Number Bonds: Subtracting 9

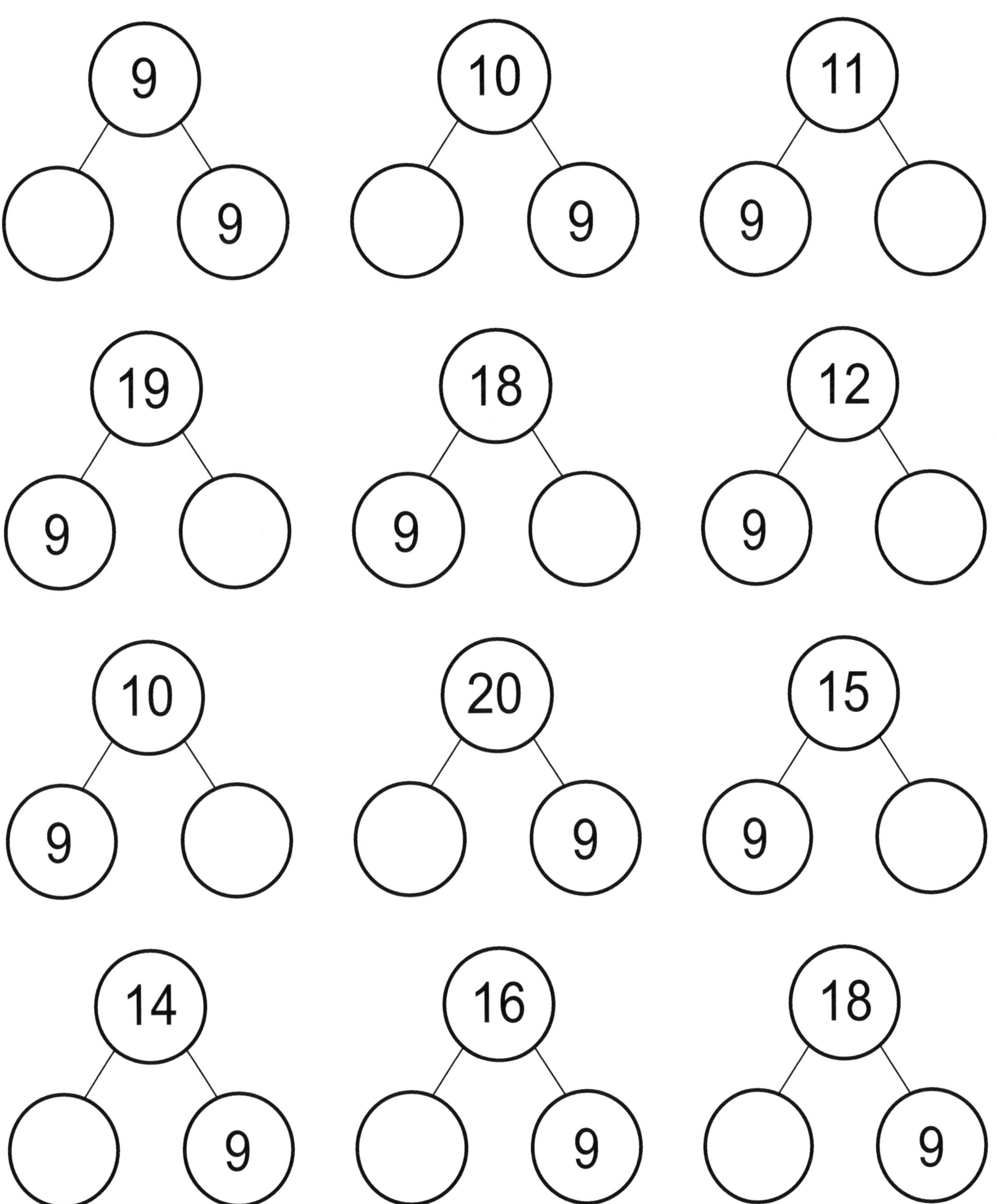

Complete the math sentences: Subtracting 9

9 - 9 = ☐

9 - ☐ = 0

☐ - 9 = 1

10 - 9 = ☐

11 - ☐ = 2

☐ - 9 = 3

12 - 9 = ☐

13 - ☐ = 4

☐ - 9 = 5

18 - 9 = ☐

19 - ☐ = 10

☐ - 9 = 6

13 - 9 = ☐

16 - 9 = ☐

Subtracting 10

$\begin{array}{r} 10 \\ -\ 10 \\ \hline \end{array}$	$\begin{array}{r} 20 \\ -\ 10 \\ \hline \end{array}$	$\begin{array}{r} 30 \\ -\ 10 \\ \hline \end{array}$	$\begin{array}{r} 40 \\ -\ 10 \\ \hline \end{array}$	$\begin{array}{r} 50 \\ -\ 10 \\ \hline \end{array}$
$\begin{array}{r} 11 \\ -\ 10 \\ \hline \end{array}$	$\begin{array}{r} 12 \\ -\ 10 \\ \hline \end{array}$	$\begin{array}{r} 13 \\ -\ 10 \\ \hline \end{array}$	$\begin{array}{r} 14 \\ -\ 10 \\ \hline \end{array}$	$\begin{array}{r} 15 \\ -\ 10 \\ \hline \end{array}$
$\begin{array}{r} 16 \\ -\ 10 \\ \hline \end{array}$	$\begin{array}{r} 17 \\ -\ 10 \\ \hline \end{array}$	$\begin{array}{r} 18 \\ -\ 10 \\ \hline \end{array}$	$\begin{array}{r} 19 \\ -\ 10 \\ \hline \end{array}$	$\begin{array}{r} 20 \\ -\ 10 \\ \hline \end{array}$
$\begin{array}{r} 11 \\ -\ 10 \\ \hline \end{array}$	$\begin{array}{r} 80 \\ -\ 10 \\ \hline \end{array}$	$\begin{array}{r} 20 \\ -\ 10 \\ \hline \end{array}$	$\begin{array}{r} 90 \\ -\ 10 \\ \hline \end{array}$	$\begin{array}{r} 40 \\ -\ 10 \\ \hline \end{array}$
$\begin{array}{r} 12 \\ -\ 10 \\ \hline \end{array}$	$\begin{array}{r} 10 \\ -\ 10 \\ \hline \end{array}$	$\begin{array}{r} 12 \\ -\ 10 \\ \hline \end{array}$	$\begin{array}{r} 16 \\ -\ 10 \\ \hline \end{array}$	$\begin{array}{r} 25 \\ -\ 10 \\ \hline \end{array}$

Number Bonds: Subtracting 10

Complete the math sentences: Subtracting 10

11 - 10 = □

10 - □ = 0

□ - 10 = 2

13 - 10 = □

11 - □ = 1

□ - 10 = 3

12 - 10 = □

14 - □ = 4

□ - 10 = 5

18 - 10 = □

19 - □ = 9

□ - 10 = 6

13 - 10 = □

16 - 10 = □

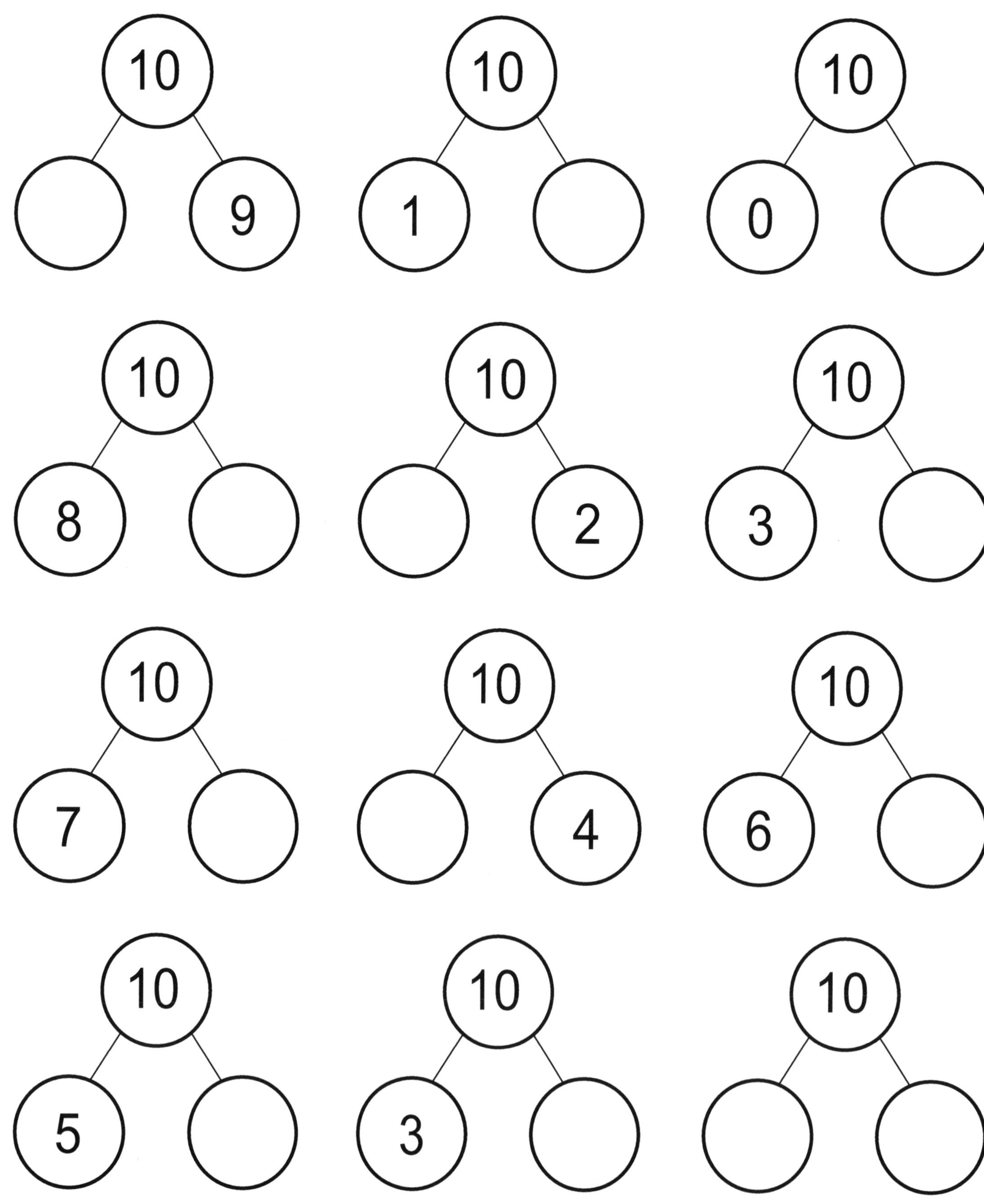
10
9
10
1
10
0
10
8
10
2
10
3
10
7
10
4
10
6
10
5
10
3
10

Review: Complete the math sentences

$10 + 3 = \square$ $\quad$ $2 + \square = 9$

$\square + 7 = 10$ $\quad$ $2 + 4 = \square$

$5 + \square = 12$ $\quad$ $\square + 3 = 9$

$4 + 3 = \square$ $\quad$ $4 + \square = 8$

$\square + 8 = 10$ $\quad$ $5 + 5 = \square$

$10 + \square = 17$ $\quad$ $\square + 2 = 7$

$8 + 3 = \square$ $\quad$ $7 + 9 = \square$

Challenge: Complete the number bond pyramid

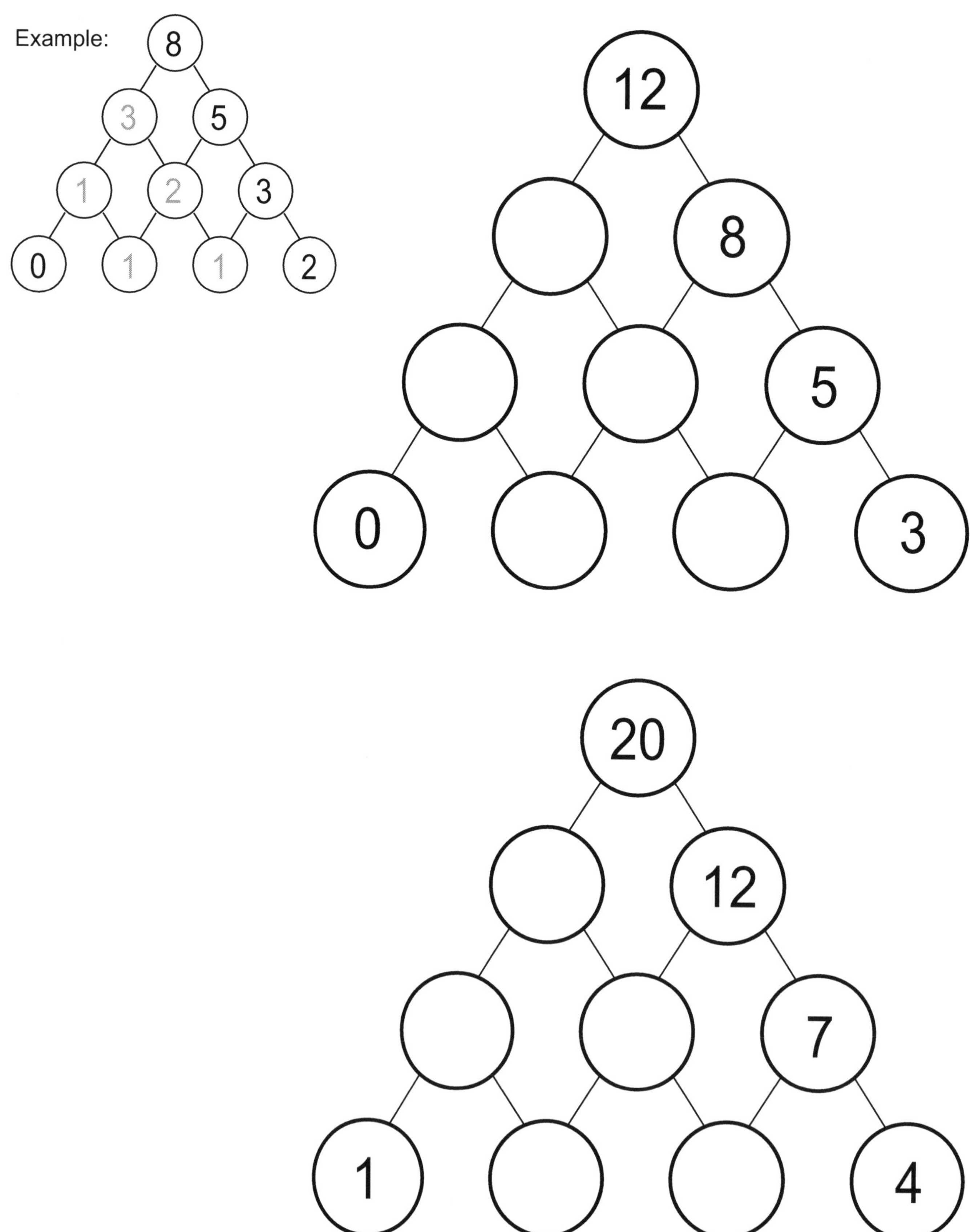

Review: Addition

2 + 3	3 + 1	2 + 4	3 + 3	4 + 3
4 + 4	5 + 4	5 + 5	6 + 5	7 + 5
7 + 2	3 + 7	10 + 2	6 + 4	5 + 6
5 + 10	9 + 3	8 + 2	9 + 5	3 + 5
8 + 8	9 + 8	9 + 9	9 + 10	10 + 10

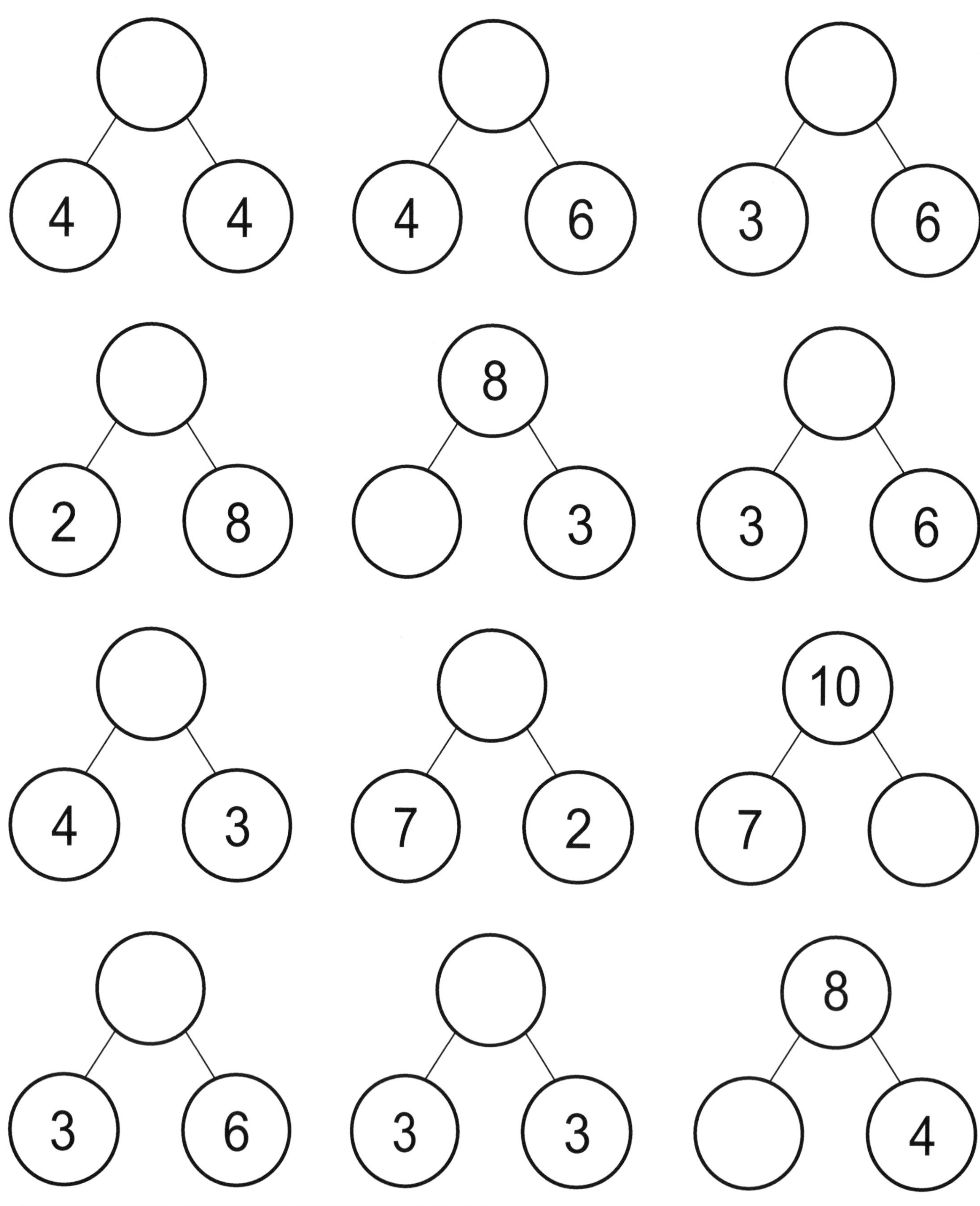
4
4
4
6
3
6
2
8
8
3
3
6
4
3
7
2
10
7
3
6
3
3
8
4

Review: Complete the math sentences

$7 + 3 = \square$

$4 + \square = 10$

$\square + 8 = 12$

$8 + 3 = \square$

$2 + \square = 10$

$\square + 3 = 8$

$4 + 2 = \square$

$5 + \square = 13$

$\square + 3 = 7$

$9 + 9 = \square$

$10 + \square = 15$

$\square + 6 = 12$

$6 + 7 = \square$

$6 + 5 = \square$

6 - 5 = ___	9 - 2 = ___	8 - 4 = ___	3 - 2 = ___	2 - 2 = ___
10 - 8 = ___	20 - 10 = ___	15 - 10 = ___	10 - 9 = ___	7 - 2 = ___
18 - 10 = ___	5 - 2 = ___	7 - 4 = ___	9 - 7 = ___	8 - 5 = ___
6 - 3 = ___	12 - 2 = ___	8 - 3 = ___	30 - 10 = ___	15 - 5 = ___
14 - 10 = ___	4 - 4 = ___	10 - 2 = ___	9 - 8 = ___	10 - 7 = ___

Review: Number Bonds

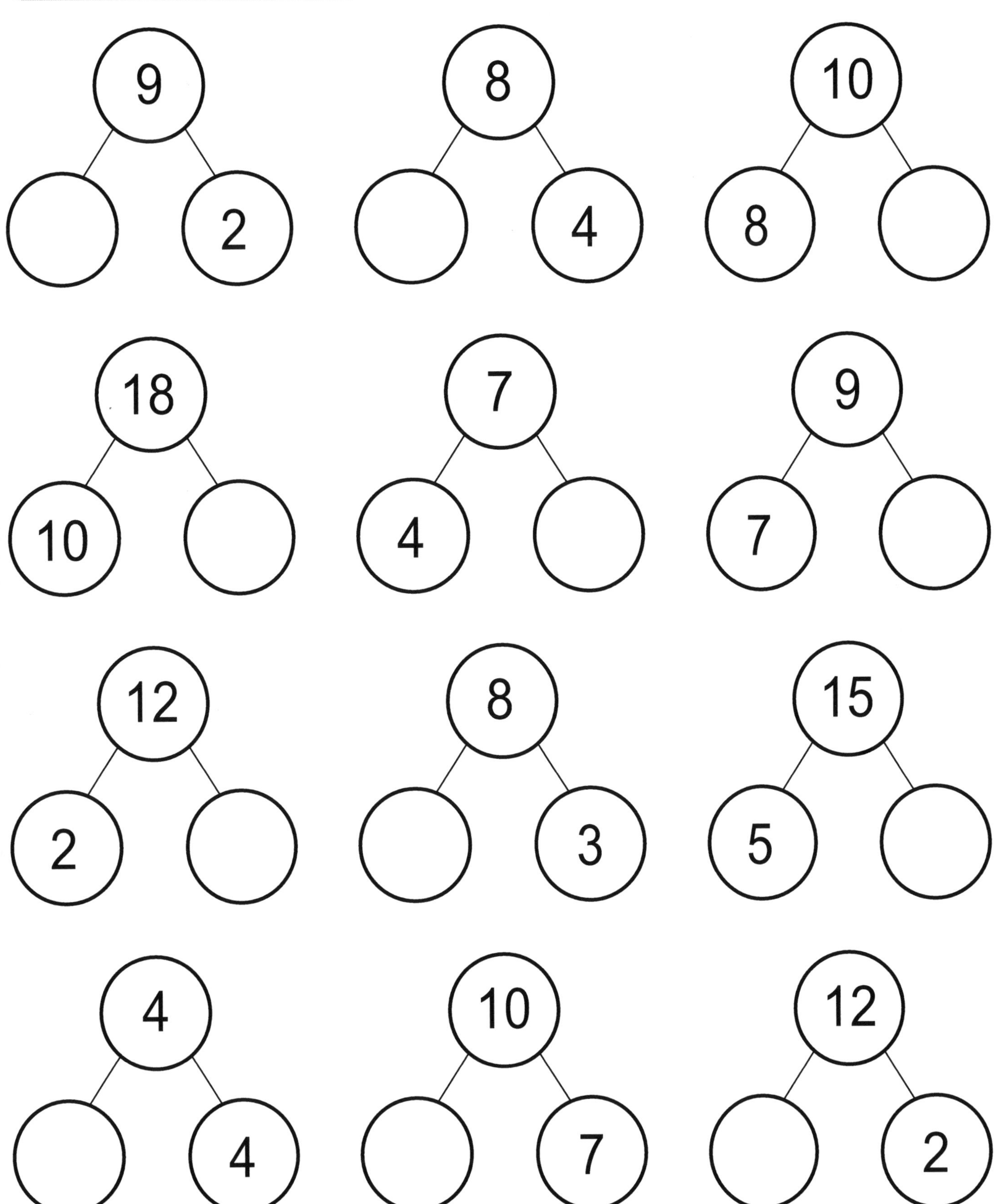

Review: Complete the math sentences

9 - 3 = □

10 - □ = 7

□ - 4 = 2

7 - 3 = □

12 - □ = 2

□ - 3 = 3

10 - 6 = □

6 - □ = 4

□ - 5 = 5

8 - 3 = □

5 - □ = 1

□ - 2 = 6

7 - 2 = □

8 - 4 = □

Review: Addition and Subtraction

$$\begin{array}{r} 4 \\ + \quad 3 \\ \hline \end{array} \qquad \begin{array}{r} 5 \\ + \quad 5 \\ \hline \end{array} \qquad \begin{array}{r} 2 \\ + \quad 6 \\ \hline \end{array} \qquad \begin{array}{r} 1 \\ + \quad 9 \\ \hline \end{array} \qquad \begin{array}{r} 8 \\ + \quad 2 \\ \hline \end{array}$$

$$\begin{array}{r} 9 \\ - \quad 2 \\ \hline \end{array} \qquad \begin{array}{r} 8 \\ - \quad 4 \\ \hline \end{array} \qquad \begin{array}{r} 7 \\ - \quad 3 \\ \hline \end{array} \qquad \begin{array}{r} 6 \\ - \quad 2 \\ \hline \end{array} \qquad \begin{array}{r} 5 \\ - \quad 4 \\ \hline \end{array}$$

$$\begin{array}{r} 7 \\ + \quad 2 \\ \hline \end{array} \qquad \begin{array}{r} 3 \\ + \quad 7 \\ \hline \end{array} \qquad \begin{array}{r} 10 \\ + \quad 1 \\ \hline \end{array} \qquad \begin{array}{r} 6 \\ + \quad 4 \\ \hline \end{array} \qquad \begin{array}{r} 6 \\ + \quad 5 \\ \hline \end{array}$$

$$\begin{array}{r} 10 \\ - \quad 5 \\ \hline \end{array} \qquad \begin{array}{r} 4 \\ - \quad 3 \\ \hline \end{array} \qquad \begin{array}{r} 5 \\ - \quad 2 \\ \hline \end{array} \qquad \begin{array}{r} 9 \\ - \quad 5 \\ \hline \end{array} \qquad \begin{array}{r} 11 \\ - \quad 10 \\ \hline \end{array}$$

$$\begin{array}{r} 1 \\ + \quad 10 \\ \hline \end{array} \qquad \begin{array}{r} 5 \\ - \quad 0 \\ \hline \end{array} \qquad \begin{array}{r} 2 \\ + \quad 2 \\ \hline \end{array} \qquad \begin{array}{r} 15 \\ - \quad 10 \\ \hline \end{array} \qquad \begin{array}{r} 20 \\ - \quad 10 \\ \hline \end{array}$$

Review: Addition and Subtraction

10 - 3 = □

4 + □ = 9

□ + 8 = 10

8 - 4 = □

12 - □ = 10

□ + 2 = 7

6 - 2 = □

5 + □ = 15

□ + 3 = 10

9 - 9 = □

10 + □ = 20

□ - 6 = 3

6 + 2 = □

10 - 5 = □

Review: Number Bonds

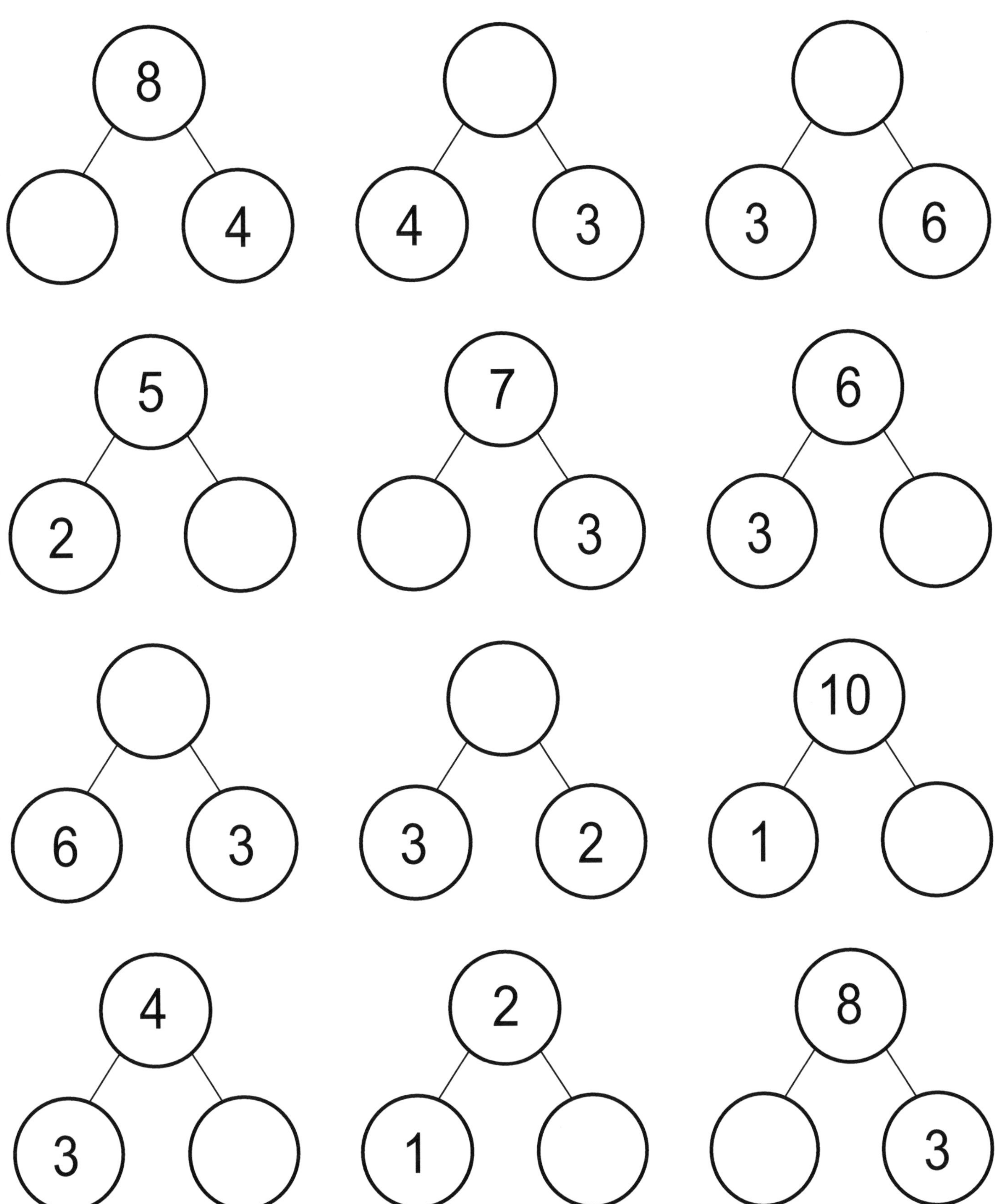

Review: Fill in the Blank

$\begin{array}{r} 4 \\ + \square \\ \hline 8 \end{array}$	$\begin{array}{r} 4 \\ + 3 \\ \hline \square \end{array}$	$\begin{array}{r} 3 \\ + 6 \\ \hline \square \end{array}$	$\begin{array}{r} \square \\ + 2 \\ \hline 5 \end{array}$	$\begin{array}{r} 3 \\ + \square \\ \hline 7 \end{array}$
$\begin{array}{r} 3 \\ + \square \\ \hline 6 \end{array}$	$\begin{array}{r} 6 \\ + 3 \\ \hline \square \end{array}$	$\begin{array}{r} 3 \\ + 2 \\ \hline \square \end{array}$	$\begin{array}{r} \square \\ + 1 \\ \hline 10 \end{array}$	$\begin{array}{r} 3 \\ + \square \\ \hline 4 \end{array}$
$\begin{array}{r} 1 \\ + \square \\ \hline 2 \end{array}$	$\begin{array}{r} 1 \\ + 5 \\ \hline \square \end{array}$	$\begin{array}{r} 2 \\ + 7 \\ \hline \square \end{array}$	$\begin{array}{r} \square \\ + 3 \\ \hline 8 \end{array}$	$\begin{array}{r} 8 \\ + \square \\ \hline 10 \end{array}$
$\begin{array}{r} 2 \\ + \square \\ \hline 5 \end{array}$	$\begin{array}{r} 4 \\ + 4 \\ \hline \square \end{array}$	$\begin{array}{r} 3 \\ + 4 \\ \hline \square \end{array}$	$\begin{array}{r} \square \\ + 4 \\ \hline 7 \end{array}$	$\begin{array}{r} 2 \\ + \square \\ \hline 9 \end{array}$
$\begin{array}{r} 5 \\ + \square \\ \hline 5 \end{array}$	$\begin{array}{r} 4 \\ + 5 \\ \hline \square \end{array}$	$\begin{array}{r} 8 \\ + 1 \\ \hline \square \end{array}$	$\begin{array}{r} \square \\ + 3 \\ \hline 9 \end{array}$	$\begin{array}{r} 3 \\ + \square \\ \hline 8 \end{array}$

Review: Addition and Subtraction

$\begin{array}{r} 3 \\ +\ 2 \\ \hline \end{array}$	$\begin{array}{r} 4 \\ +\ 4 \\ \hline \end{array}$	$\begin{array}{r} 2 \\ +\ 5 \\ \hline \end{array}$	$\begin{array}{r} 7 \\ +\ 0 \\ \hline \end{array}$	$\begin{array}{r} 7 \\ +\ 1 \\ \hline \end{array}$
$\begin{array}{r} 8 \\ -\ 1 \\ \hline \end{array}$	$\begin{array}{r} 7 \\ -\ 3 \\ \hline \end{array}$	$\begin{array}{r} 6 \\ -\ 2 \\ \hline \end{array}$	$\begin{array}{r} 5 \\ -\ 2 \\ \hline \end{array}$	$\begin{array}{r} 5 \\ -\ 5 \\ \hline \end{array}$
$\begin{array}{r} 9 \\ +\ 1 \\ \hline \end{array}$	$\begin{array}{r} 2 \\ +\ 9 \\ \hline \end{array}$	$\begin{array}{r} 10 \\ +\ 3 \\ \hline \end{array}$	$\begin{array}{r} 10 \\ +\ 4 \\ \hline \end{array}$	$\begin{array}{r} 9 \\ +\ 5 \\ \hline \end{array}$
$\begin{array}{r} 9 \\ -\ 5 \\ \hline \end{array}$	$\begin{array}{r} 3 \\ -\ 3 \\ \hline \end{array}$	$\begin{array}{r} 3 \\ -\ 2 \\ \hline \end{array}$	$\begin{array}{r} 9 \\ -\ 2 \\ \hline \end{array}$	$\begin{array}{r} 15 \\ -\ 10 \\ \hline \end{array}$
$\begin{array}{r} 10 \\ +\ 10 \\ \hline \end{array}$	$\begin{array}{r} 6 \\ -\ 4 \\ \hline \end{array}$	$\begin{array}{r} 3 \\ +\ 3 \\ \hline \end{array}$	$\begin{array}{r} 25 \\ -\ 10 \\ \hline \end{array}$	$\begin{array}{r} 50 \\ -\ 10 \\ \hline \end{array}$

$10 - 3 = \square$

$4 + \square = 9$

$\square + 8 = 10$

$8 - 4 = \square$

$12 - \square = 10$

$\square + 2 = 7$

$6 - 2 = \square$

$5 + \square = 15$

$\square + 3 = 10$

$9 - 9 = \square$

$10 + \square = 20$

$\square - 6 = 3$

$6 + 2 = \square$

$10 - 5 = \square$

Review: Number Bonds

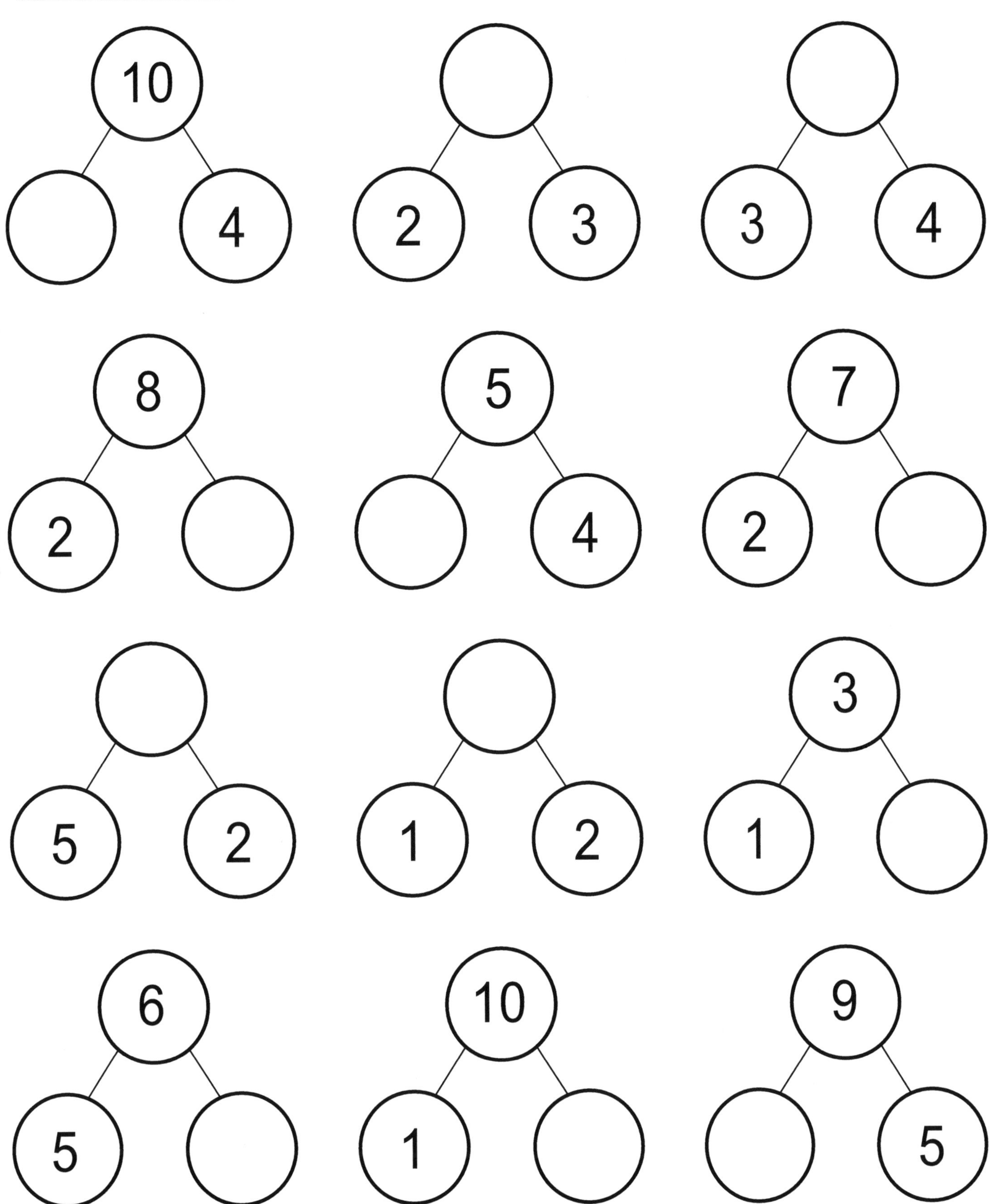

Review: Fill in the Blank

$4 + \square = 10$ | $2 + 3 = \square$ | $3 + 4 = \square$ | $\square + 2 = 8$ | $4 + \square = 5$

$2 + \square = 7$ | $5 + 2 = \square$ | $2 + 1 = \square$ | $\square + 1 = 3$ | $5 + \square = 6$

$1 + \square = 10$ | $2 + 4 = \square$ | $3 + 5 = \square$ | $\square + 3 = 4$ | $5 + \square = 9$

$4 + \square = 8$ | $4 + 5 = \square$ | $5 + 5 = \square$ | $\square + 4 = 9$ | $3 + \square = 8$

$5 + \square = 10$ | $4 + 7 = \square$ | $8 + 4 = \square$ | $\square + 4 = 10$ | $9 + \square = 10$

Challenge: Complete the number bond pyramid

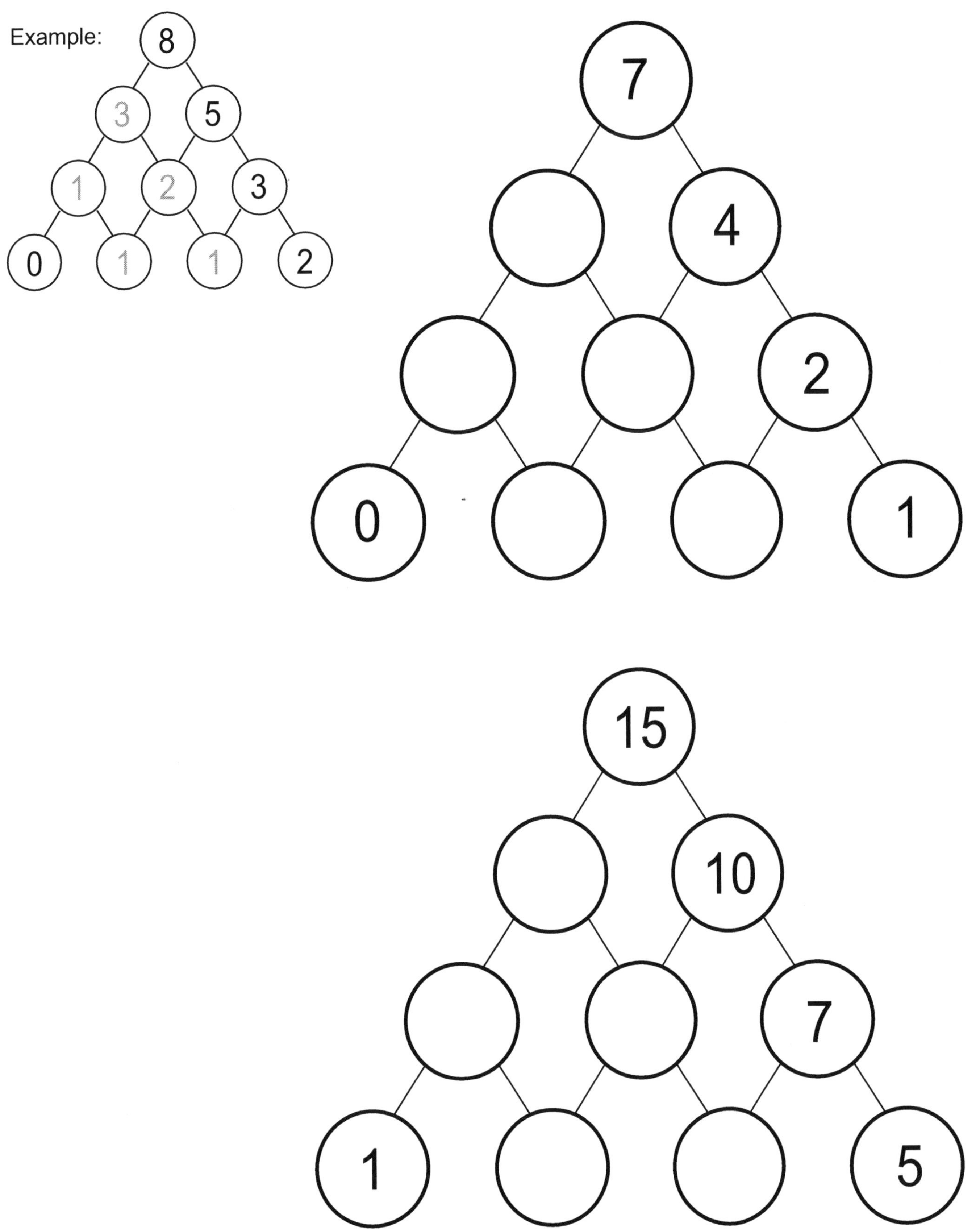

Challenge: Addition

10 + 3	10 + 5	15 + 5	20 + 10	20 + 15
9 + 2	8 + 4	7 + 5	9 + 7	6 + 7
12 + 3	7 + 9	12 + 10	6 + 8	9 + 5
5 + 5	6 + 6	7 + 7	8 + 8	9 + 9
10 + 10	25 + 10	30 + 15	40 + 40	50 + 30

Challenge: Number Bonds

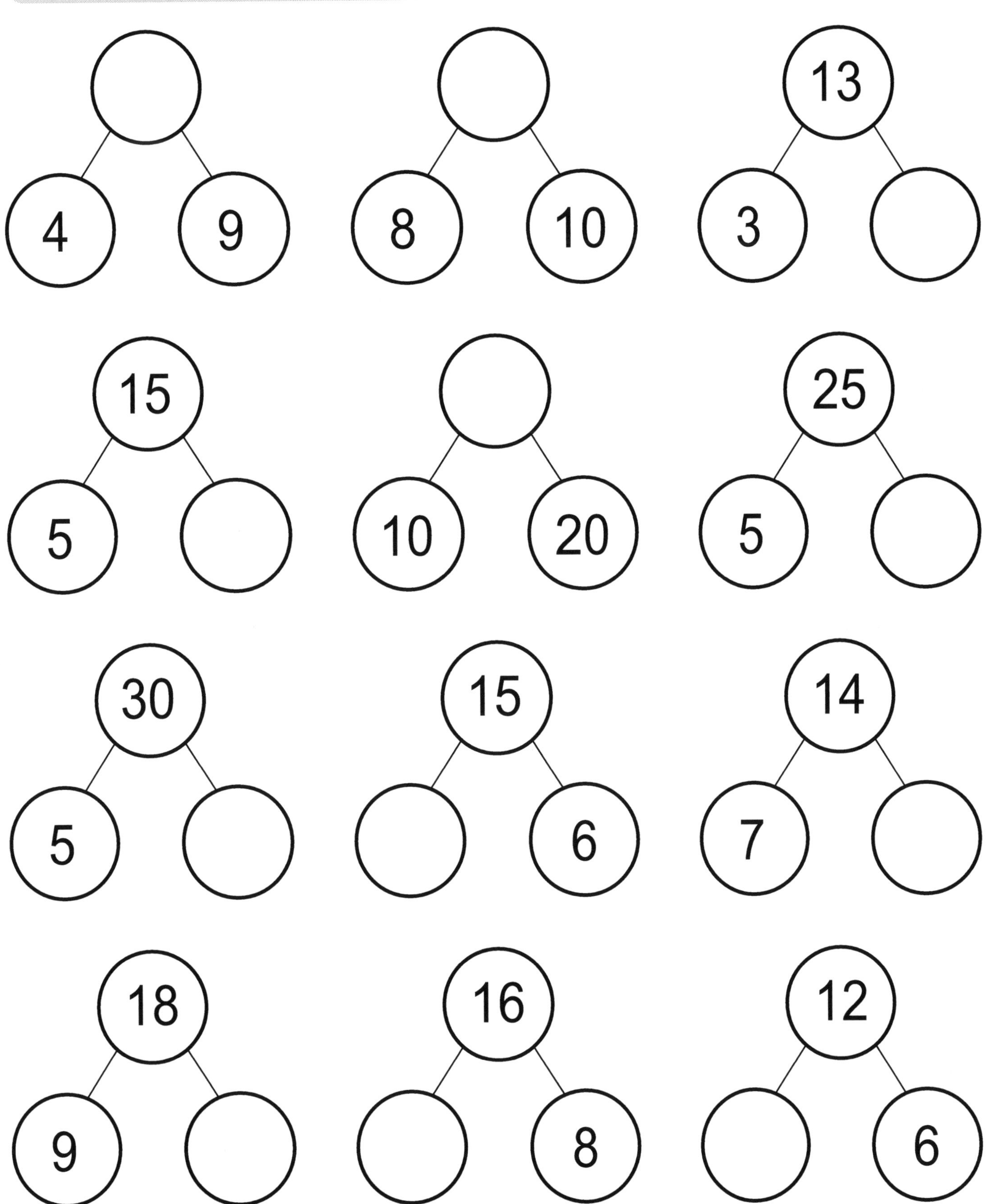

Challenge: Complete the math sentences

$10 + 10 = \square$

$10 + \square = 25$

$\square + 7 = 27$

$25 + 10 = \square$

$25 + \square = 35$

$\square + 12 = 20$

$16 + 4 = \square$

$9 + \square = 18$

$\square + 8 = 16$

$7 + 7 = \square$

$10 + \square = 60$

$\square + 18 = 20$

$8 + 13 = \square$

$7 + 14 = \square$

Challenge: Subtraction

$10 - 5$	$15 - 5$	$20 - 10$	$11 - 6$	$12 - 7$
$15 - 8$	$20 - 8$	$16 - 8$	$14 - 7$	$12 - 6$
$19 - 9$	$18 - 9$	$13 - 4$	$14 - 6$	$16 - 9$
$20 - 9$	$25 - 5$	$35 - 15$	$22 - 12$	$11 - 8$
$12 - 8$	$17 - 7$	$17 - 8$	$17 - 9$	$17 - 10$

Challenge: Complete the math sentences

15 - 10 = ☐

10 - ☐ = 2

☐ - 7 = 10

18 - 9 = ☐

20 - ☐ = 12

☐ - 2 = 2

16 - 12 = ☐

9 - ☐ = 4

☐ - 8 = 7

14 - 7 = ☐

30 - ☐ = 20

☐ - 12 = 8

13 - 8 = ☐

18 - 4 = ☐

Challenge: Addition and Subtraction Fill in the Blank

$\begin{array}{r} 4 \\ + \square \\ \hline 14 \end{array}$	$\begin{array}{r} 10 \\ - 3 \\ \hline \square \end{array}$	$\begin{array}{r} 8 \\ + 6 \\ \hline \square \end{array}$	$\begin{array}{r} \square \\ - 2 \\ \hline 7 \end{array}$	$\begin{array}{r} 9 \\ - \square \\ \hline 5 \end{array}$
$\begin{array}{r} 10 \\ - \square \\ \hline 7 \end{array}$	$\begin{array}{r} 15 \\ + 5 \\ \hline \square \end{array}$	$\begin{array}{r} 10 \\ - 3 \\ \hline \square \end{array}$	$\begin{array}{r} \square \\ + 3 \\ \hline 15 \end{array}$	$\begin{array}{r} 15 \\ - \square \\ \hline 6 \end{array}$
$\begin{array}{r} 6 \\ + \square \\ \hline 12 \end{array}$	$\begin{array}{r} 12 \\ - 6 \\ \hline \square \end{array}$	$\begin{array}{r} 15 \\ - 9 \\ \hline \square \end{array}$	$\begin{array}{r} \square \\ + 3 \\ \hline 8 \end{array}$	$\begin{array}{r} 12 \\ + \square \\ \hline 15 \end{array}$
$\begin{array}{r} 20 \\ - \square \\ \hline 8 \end{array}$	$\begin{array}{r} 12 \\ + 8 \\ \hline \square \end{array}$	$\begin{array}{r} 9 \\ + 9 \\ \hline \square \end{array}$	$\begin{array}{r} \square \\ - 1 \\ \hline 9 \end{array}$	$\begin{array}{r} 10 \\ - \square \\ \hline 8 \end{array}$
$\begin{array}{r} 8 \\ + \square \\ \hline 10 \end{array}$	$\begin{array}{r} 14 \\ - 7 \\ \hline \square \end{array}$	$\begin{array}{r} 8 \\ + 7 \\ \hline \square \end{array}$	$\begin{array}{r} \square \\ - 4 \\ \hline 10 \end{array}$	$\begin{array}{r} 20 \\ - \square \\ \hline 10 \end{array}$

Make Your Own Number Bonds

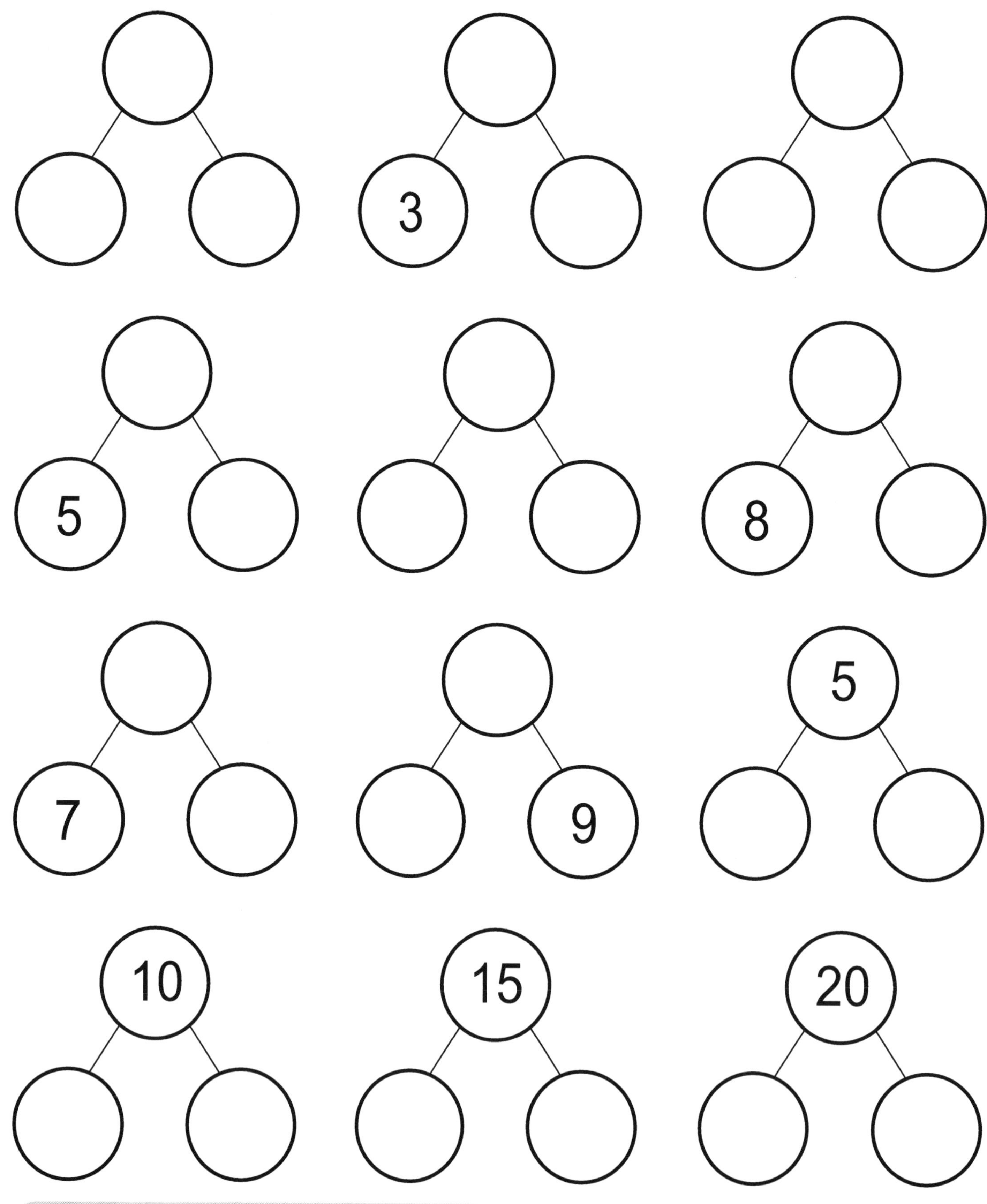

Make Your Own Number Bonds

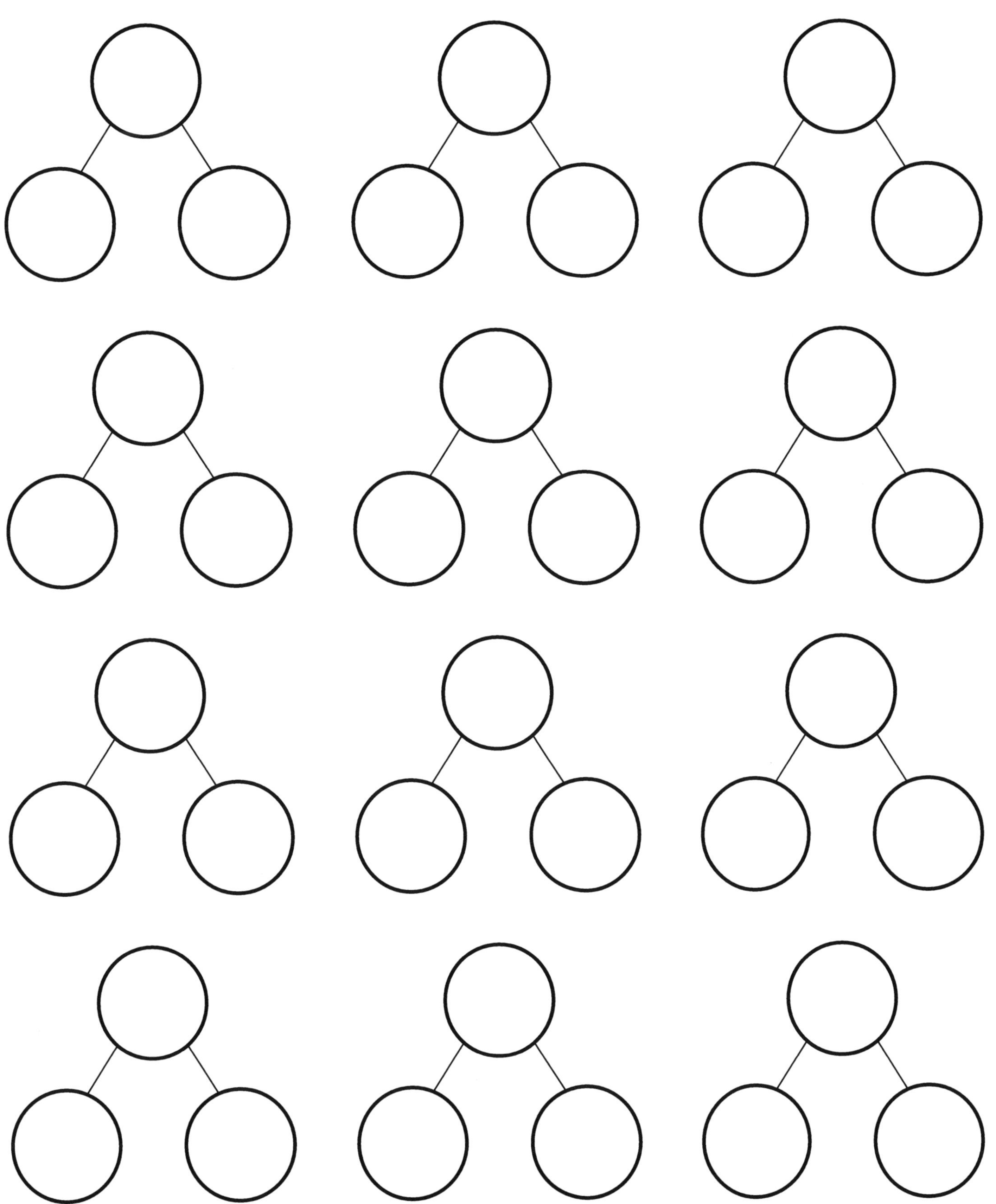

Make your own number bond pyramid

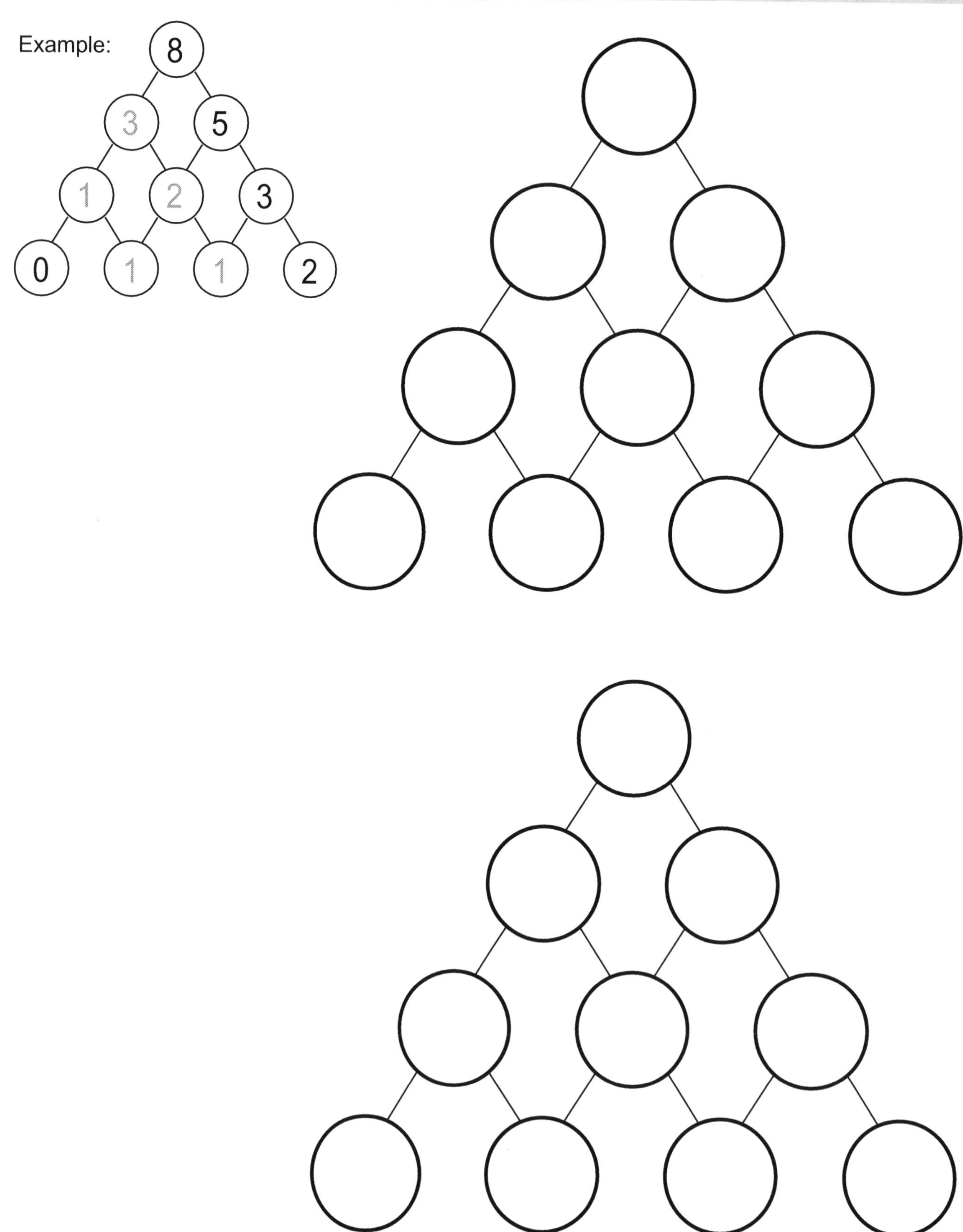

Where are the answers?

We know kids will peek at the answers at the back of workbooks, so we are not including answers at the back of this book on purpose. For a pdf of the answer key, go to www.numberbondgames.com/books

If you liked this book...

Please leave us a 5 star review on Amazon, and check out other books by Elita Nathan and our new Race to Planet X Number Bond Board Game.

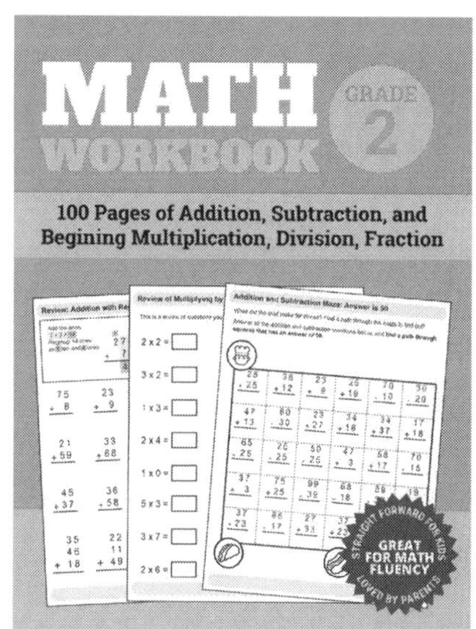

Math Workbook Grade 2: 100 Pages of Addition, Subtraction and Beginning Multiplication, Division, Fraction by Elita Nathan

- The next Math Workbook in the series!
- Math Workbook Grade 2 continues to build on key foundational mathematics basics: addition, subtraction, and introduction to multiplication, division, and fraction.
- Note: Many schools do not start multiplication or division until 3rd grade, but we are covering these concepts here since it does take time and practice to get comfortable with multiplication and division.

Race To Planet X

Number Bond Game

- Award winning educational math board game that is actually fun to play
- Have fun while practicing addition and subtraction 1-20
- Strengthen and reinforce number bond concepts taught in elementary schools. Ideal for 5-8 years old.

ages 5+
2-4 players
15 mins

Congratulations!

____

has completed 100 pages of math problems

____

Date

Manufactured by Amazon.ca
Bolton, ON

23918637R00059